# MEALS TO ENJOY FROM YOUR FREEZER

Audrey Ellis

**HAMLYN**
LONDON · NEW · YORK · SYDNEY · TORONTO

Books by the same author:

All About Home Freezing
Step by Step Guide to Home Freezing
Entertaining from your Freezer
Complete Book of Home Freezing

Published by
The Hamlyn Publishing Group Limited
London · New York · Sydney · Toronto
Astronaut House, Feltham, Middlesex, England
© Copyright The Hamlyn Publishing Group Limited 1969
First published 1969
Sixth impression 1974
Revised edition 1974
ISBN 0 600 36164 0
Printed in England by Fleetway Printers, Gravesend, Kent

# Contents

*Front cover illustration shows*
*Chicken Kiev, page 28*
*and Strawberry soufflé, page 66*

The author gratefully acknowledges the help of:
RESEARCH EDITORS: GWYNEDD HINDMARSH & ANN SCUTCHER
Special series of food preparation photographs taken by:
Butter Information Council
Ann Smith and Frigidaire Division of General Motors Limited
Blue Band Bureau
Birds Eye Foods Limited
Fruit Producers' Council
The Tupperware Company

# Introduction

In response to numerous requests, the publishers have decided to reproduce *Home Guide to Deep Freezing* as two paper-back volumes.

The first volume, under the title *All About Home Freezing*, deals with choosing, buying and filling a freezer. This second volume, which has been considerably expanded, contains advice on menu-planning and many recipes for appetising meals from the freezer.

There are three advantages which, when you invest in a freezer, you will soon discover.

Firstly, you will be able to buy commercially frozen food and fresh meat in bulk at considerably reduced prices and save a substantial sum month by month towards the initial cost of the freezer. Deliveries made to your door by refrigerated van will make frequent shopping expeditions a thing of the past, saving your money, time and energy.

Secondly, freezing your own garden produce, or fresh fruit and vegetables you can buy cheaply at certain times of the year, will represent another economy. You will find that you always have plenty of food in stock and your first reaction when planning meals for the day soon tends to be – 'What is in my freezer?' rather than – 'What must I buy today?' But there is a further bonus in time and money saved by the use of the freezer for preserving home-cooked dishes.

The average housewife spends more time each day cooking than in any other task. Breakfast, packed meals, elevenses, lunch, tea, dinner, suppers and snacks – there seems no end to the number of meals to be prepared each day and no escape from the kitchen for the harassed housewife. Cooking always seems to coincide with other important domestic chores, just when you are busiest – getting the children off to school, helping them with their homework, or putting the little ones to bed! Or if you are a working wife, it seems to swallow up all your spare time.

This is where the freezer can help you to plan and cook ahead. A great deal of time can be saved in repetitive preparation tasks by cooking in much larger quantities and freezing a number of meals for future use, as well as having one ready to eat at once. You can do most of your cooking at the time of day when you are free to give your whole attention to it. Many housewives seem to find that this is during the early afternoon, by the way, but working wives often prefer to have a big cooking spree over the weekend.

In fact, by partly stocking your freezer with cooked dishes which will include pre-cooked sauces and prepared items such as uncooked pastry and biscuit dough, you can alter the entire pattern of catering for the family to reduce the hard work involved to an absolute minimum.

You will find chain cooking, which is fully described in Chapter Two, is another fascinating adventure in cooking for a freezer owner.

It is such a boon to have stocks of your own home-made sauces always available, to dress up a pasta dish or transform left-overs into a creamy ragoût. Just see how many ready-to-cook and fully prepared dishes you can chain-cook with chicken, for example. One cake-making session each month will keep the family well supplied with delicious fresh cakes, even elaborate iced ones. And one sandwich-making session will cover all demands for packed meals, even rations for the children's friends who drop in to play and stay over tea-time.

It is a good idea to make up packs of assorted sandwiches for freezing. If someone has a special preference or dislike, write his name on packs which contain no peanut butter, or plenty of sardine spread, according to individual taste. Sandwiches take about $2\frac{1}{2}$ hours to thaw, which means that they're usually just ready for eating by the time they're needed. If needed more quickly, spread them on a plate to thaw.

You will soon become accustomed to the convenience of serving commercially frozen foods more often because buying them in bulk is more economical. You may then feel like experimenting to find new, adventurous ways of serving them.

It is now so much easier to find suppliers of bulk frozen foods who will give you a very prompt, reasonable and satisfactory service, no matter where you live, that I have felt it necessary to include a special new chapter on making more of these convenience foods.

Various different services are rapidly becoming available to housewives who want to buy some or most household items in bulk, and take advantage of the big savings this kind of buying makes possible. You may like to buy only frozen products such as fruit, vegetables, pastry and prepared dishes, and there is now the excellent Birds Eye Home Freezer Service throughout the country to suit your needs. Other firms supply ready frozen products, plus butcher's meat, and sometimes even wine in bulk, and also offer freezers at a worthwhile discount. Bejam Bulk Buying give this very full type of service and now have over 70 branches.

The freezer is a true friend to every housewife who tries (however spasmodically) to follow a slimming diet. It is all too easy to fill up on bread, rolls or biscuits when no more suitable food is available, but it is just the food dieters need which occupies most space in the freezer. Fruit, vegetables, meat, poultry – you can even freeze individual portions of cooked lean meat and chicken specially labelled for yourself, prepared without any starchy ingredients. This method comes in handy when any member of the family is temporarily (or always as in the case of a diabetic, or a person with a constant weight problem) on a special diet. You can keep a supply of food on hand specially labelled and parcelled, to enable you to serve this one person an entirely different meal with the minimum of trouble.

You may also find it handy to make use of a special one-portion pack for someone who has to eat at different times from the rest of the household. Sometimes unusual working hours, or a hobby that keeps someone away from family meal-times, causes this problem. When you have a big cooking spree, you could very easily fill a batch of foil dinner plates with individual portions of a meat or poultry dish.

Entertaining one's friends ought to be a pleasure but many housewives secretly feel that the enjoyment is very much diminished by the additional hard work and anxiety involved in catering. It embarrasses any hostess to let her guests see that preparing a meal for them is really a chore. It may well deprive them of her company for a good deal of their visit. With a choice of ready-cooked food always to hand in your freezer it is much more of a pleasure to cater for guests, even unexpected ones.

Big parties, where there is a lot of food to prepare, often leave the hostess too exhausted and harassed to enjoy herself. Where there is storage space available in the freezer, many dishes can be made during leisure hours, days or even more than a week beforehand. This applies to fancy sandwiches, canapés, hors-d'oeuvre and soups as well as main dishes and sweets. If you prepare more than is needed you can cut down on wastage by keeping extra supplies in the refrigerator and returning them to the freezer if they are not needed. If dinner-party guests cancel on the day, you have a wonderful meal in store which need not be used for months to come; or, it can be served to guests you did not expect, tomorrow.

To sum up, careful use of the freezer should enable you to save time and money and enjoy a far greater range of menus than ever before. It is particularly rewarding when you have made a good 'buy' and at the same time provided trouble-free meals for weeks or even months ahead. But the amount of time and effort you save is undoubtedly governed by forethought and planning on your part.

Audrey Ellis

**Chapter One**

# Cooking ahead – the 'eat one, freeze two' plan

This section is devoted entirely to providing food for the day-to-day needs of the family. All of the king-size recipes found here are intended to give three complete meals, each one large enough to serve a family of four people. They can easily be adapted to meet your own particular needs – increasing the amounts by half as much again, for example, if yours is a family of six.

## Cooking in bulk

The most workable plan seems to be to cook your main meal requirements once a week by preparing two main dishes, each in sufficient quantity to serve four people three times. This will make a total of six complete meals for four people. One meal, say a liver casserole, is served straight away: a second meal, perhaps using lamb chops, will be refrigerated until it can be eaten the next day; which leaves four meals, two of each kind, to be frozen. You will already have a good assortment of meals in the freezer so that you can choose from these for the rest of the week, ensuring that you don't have to eat liver casserole and lamb chops the whole week through!

It is a good notion to give each complete meal a slight variation before freezing – or eating – it. If you make a steak and kidney casserole, you can give that day's meal a pastry crust, and the two meals destined for the freezer can be given trimmings to make them a little different (for example, cobbler topping).

You will already have noticed that six meals are prepared each week, while there are seven days to be dealt with! This isn't an oversight, but it has been assumed that on at least one day out of every week, you will be invited to someone else's home for a meal, or perhaps friends will be coming to you, in which case you will not be feeding them from the family-meal section of the freezer. Your husband might unexpectedly take you out to a restaurant meal or bring home something for dinner!

The dishes you decide to prepare and freeze each week can depend on the foodstuffs that happen to be a particularly good buy at the time. For example, chicken or lamb dishes when they are especially cheap. Many people are often deterred from buying big, deliciously juicy cuts of ham and gammon because they feel that they are going to be eating ham for days on end. Now you can buy and cook it, eat some of the ham straight away and freeze the remainder, made into all kinds of interesting dishes.

Soup is another wonderful family stand-by and nothing you buy, however good, is quite the equivalent of home-made soup. Serve it with hot toast and home-made pâté for a family lunch or supper.

Desserts can be whipped out of the freezer in no time – frozen purées are excellent for emergency desserts, so too is frozen fruit, which can be served with little cupcakes also stored in the freezer.

Individual dinners find their place in this section, for sometimes a member of the family is going to eat a solitary meal – either because he is going to be late or because everyone else has gone out! Use small quantities left over from bulk cooking for single portions, packed in foil plates. Incidentally it may be a little expensive to invest in aluminium foil plates for individual plate dinners, but if they are carefully treated they can be re-used and so minimise the cost.

## Green summer soup

1 oz./25 g. butter
1 small bunch spring onions, chopped
3 sticks celery, chopped
8 oz./225 g. leaf spinach
1 Webbs Wonder lettuce, shredded
1 pint/6 dl. chicken stock

Melt the butter and sauté the spring onions and celery until softened but not coloured. Add the spinach, stir well and cook for about 5 minutes. Add the lettuce and stock to the pan and bring to the boil, stirring constantly. Cover and simmer for 10 minutes. Cool, then liquidise or sieve.

**To freeze:** Pack into three plastic containers. Seal and freeze.

**To prepare for serving:** Hold the container under running cold water and turn the contents into a large saucepan. Add twice the quantity of chicken stock and reheat, stirring occasionally. Taste and correct seasonings. Or, add one part stock and one part béchamel sauce to give a creamy textured soup. *Makes 3 servings for 4.*

## Winter vegetable soup

4 sticks celery, thinly sliced
8 oz./225 g. parsnips, cut into $\frac{1}{4}$-inch/$\frac{1}{2}$-cm. dice
8 oz./225 g. turnips, cut into $\frac{1}{4}$-inch/$\frac{1}{2}$-cm. dice
2 onions, peeled and finely sliced
bouquet garni plus 6 peppercorns
4 pints/2$\frac{1}{4}$ litres chicken stock or 4 stock cubes and water
4 oz./100 g. mushrooms, finely sliced

Put all the vegetables, except the mushrooms, into a saucepan. Tie the bouquet garni and peppercorns in muslin and place in the pan. Add the stock and simmer for 20 minutes. Add the mushrooms and continue to simmer for another 10 minutes.

**To freeze:** Cool and remove the herbs. Pack into 1$\frac{1}{2}$-pint (1-litre) containers, leaving a $\frac{1}{2}$–1-inch (1–2$\frac{1}{2}$-cm.) headspace.

**To prepare for serving:** Immerse the container in hot water to remove the contents. Reheat gently in a covered saucepan. Dilute, if liked. Correct the seasoning. *Makes 3 servings for 4.*

## Buckling pâté

3 large bucklings
6 oz./175 g. butter, softened
1 clove garlic, crushed
juice of 2 lemons
freshly ground pepper

Put the bucklings in boiling water for 1 minute, so that the skin can be removed easily. Remove the skin and bones. Pound the flesh with a wooden spoon and blend together with the butter. Add the crushed garlic and lemon juice. Season to taste.

**To freeze:** Put the pâté into three foil dishes, smooth the tops and seal with a double thickness of foil.

**To prepare for serving:** Thaw at room temperature, for 3–4 hours. Turn out of the container and cut into quarters. Serve with toast. *Makes 3 servings for 4.*

## Country pâté

12 oz./350 g. pigs' liver
8 oz./225 g. fat bacon
1 onion, peeled and chopped
1 clove garlic, chopped
2 oz./50 g. butter
salt and pepper to taste
$\frac{1}{2}$ pint/3 dl. well-seasoned white sauce

Fry the liver, bacon, onion and garlic in the butter for about 10 minutes, gently. Remove from the heat and mince or put in a blender. Season with salt and pepper. Combine the liver mixture with the sauce. Turn into a 1$\frac{1}{2}$-pint (1-litre) greased terrine or pie dish, cover with a lid or foil and place in a baking tin of hot water. Bake in a moderate oven (350°F., 180°C., Gas Mark 4) for 1 hour. Cover with foil, stand kitchen weights on top and leave overnight in the refrigerator.

**To freeze:** Turn out of the dish, cut into slices and stack with pieces of foil between slices. Wrap in double or heavy duty foil. Seal and freeze.

**To prepare for serving:** Unwrap the required number of slices. Allow about 1 hour for thawing. Serve with hot toast. *Makes 3 servings for 4.*

# Chicken liver pâté

3 oz./75 g. butter
12 oz./350 g. chicken livers
salt and pepper to taste
$\frac{1}{4}$ teaspoon powdered mace

Melt 1 oz. (25 g.) of the butter in a frying pan, add the chicken livers and cook gently for 5 minutes. Pass the livers through a fine mincer, melt the remaining butter and add to the chicken livers with the rest of the ingredients.

**To freeze:** Press into three foil pie dishes and seal with double or heavy duty foil, or store individual portions using the following method: Chill the pâté in the refrigerator, turn out of the foil pie dishes and cut into quarters. Stack the slices with dividing pieces of foil or sheets of polythene tissue paper between each. Wrap in foil and seal.

**To prepare for serving:** Thaw, covered, at room temperature for approximately 1 hour. *Makes 3 servings for 4.*


# Bacon pâté

3 oz./75 g. butter
1 large onion, finely chopped
1$\frac{1}{2}$ lb./675 g. cooked bacon, minced
1 tablespoon chopped parsley, blanched
1 tablespoon freshly made mustard
$\frac{1}{2}$ teaspoon Worcestershire sauce

Melt the butter in a saucepan and gently fry the onion in it. Combine with the remaining ingredients. Spread the mixture evenly in a 2-lb. (1-kg.) loaf tin, smooth the top and chill in the refrigerator for 2 hours.

**To freeze:** Turn the pâté out of the loaf tin. Cut into 12 slices and stack with foil dividers between the slices. Wrap in double or heavy duty foil, seal and freeze.

**To prepare for serving:** Take the required number of slices out of the package. Thaw at room temperature allowing approximately 1 hour. *Makes 3 servings for 4.*

# Barbecued meat sauce

4 medium onions, peeled and chopped
3 cloves garlic, crushed
1 head celery, trimmed and chopped
2 oz./50 g. lard or dripping
4 lb./1$\frac{3}{4}$ kg. minced beef
4 teaspoons salt
$\frac{1}{2}$ teaspoon pepper
3 tablespoons Worcestershire sauce
$\frac{3}{4}$ pint/4 dl. tomato ketchup

Fry the onion, garlic and celery gently in the fat in a large pan. Gradually add the minced beef and stir until all the meat has browned. Add the salt, pepper, Worcestershire sauce and ketchup. Simmer gently for 20 minutes. Skim off any excess fat.

**To freeze:** Cool quickly. Spoon the mixture into three 1$\frac{1}{2}$-pint (1-litre) containers. Seal, label and freeze.

**To prepare for serving:** Immerse the container in hot water, to allow the mixture to slip out of the container into a pan for heating. This sauce can be served with all types of pasta or with rice to make a main meal. It can be heated while the rice or pasta is cooking. *Makes 4$\frac{1}{2}$ pints (2$\frac{1}{2}$ litres).*


# Barbecue sauce

2 oz./50 g. butter
2 large onions, peeled and chopped
8 tablespoons Worcestershire sauce
8 tablespoons cider or wine vinegar
2 tablespoons brown table sauce
2 oz./50 g. sugar
2 pints/generous litre water

Melt the butter in a saucepan and sauté the onion. Add the other ingredients and simmer, covered, for 20 minutes. Uncover, then boil rapidly to reduce by one third.

**To freeze:** Cool. Strain into three $\frac{1}{2}$-pint (3-dl.) containers.

**To prepare for serving:** Immerse the container in hot water. Turn out into a saucepan, simmer gently. *Makes 1$\frac{1}{2}$ pints (scant litre).*

## Taramasalata

12 oz./350 g. smoked cod's roe
½ pint/3 dl. olive oil
juice of 1 lemon
freshly ground black pepper
1 teaspoon very finely chopped onion
2 tablespoons chopped parsley, blanched

Remove the skin from the roe and discard. Put the roe in a bowl with 5 tablespoons of the oil. Allow to stand for 10 minutes. Pass the mixture through a fine sieve or liquidise in a blender. Add the lemon juice. Beat in the remaining olive oil, 1 tablespoon at a time. Add the remaining ingredients.

**To freeze:** Pack into individual foil pie dishes. Smooth the tops and seal with double or heavy duty foil. Freeze.

**To prepare for serving:** Thaw at room temperature allowing approximately 1 hour. Serve on toast as an appetiser or savoury. *Makes 3 servings for 4.*

## Tomato sauce

1 medium onion, chopped
2 cloves garlic, crushed with 1 teaspoon salt
1 tablespoon oil
3 tablespoons tomato purée
2 2 lb. 3-oz./992-g. cans tomatoes
2 tablespoons castor sugar
3–4 parsley stalks
1 bay leaf
salt and pepper to taste

Sauté the onion and garlic in the oil until soft. Stir in the tomato purée, canned tomatoes (with the juice) and sugar. Tie the parsley stalks and bay leaf with thread and add to the ingredients in the pan; add the salt and pepper. Bring to the boil, reduce the heat then cover with a lid and simmer gently for 45 minutes. Remove the parsley stalks and bay leaf.

**To freeze:** Cool rapidly. Pour into suitable containers, allowing a 1-inch (2½-cm.) headspace. Cover and freeze.

**To prepare for serving:** Reheat in a covered saucepan, over gentle heat. *Makes 4 pints (2¼ litres).*

## Curry sauce

3 tablespoons cooking oil
2 large onions, peeled and finely chopped
2 cloves garlic, crushed with 1 teaspoon salt
3 tablespoons tomato purée
2 tablespoons curry powder
2 teaspoons curry paste
1 tablespoon brown sugar
2 tablespoons mango chutney, chopped
1 11-oz./312-g. can tomatoes
1 bay leaf
1 pint/6 dl. stock or stock and gravy, mixed

Heat the oil in a saucepan, add the onions and garlic and cook gently until soft but not brown. Stir in the tomato purée, curry powder and curry paste, cook for 2 minutes. Add the remaining ingredients, cover with a lid and simmer for 45 minutes.

**To freeze:** Cool and pack into ½-pint (3-dl.) plastic containers, leaving a ½-inch (1-cm.) headspace. Seal and freeze.

**To prepare for serving:** Immerse in hot water to loosen the contents. Reheat gently in a saucepan. Use for curried eggs, chicken or vegetables. *Makes approximately 1½ pints (scant litre).*

## Onion sauce

1 lb./450 g. onions, peeled and chopped
2 tablespoons cornflour
½ pint/3 dl. milk
1 chicken stock cube

Put the onions in a saucepan, cover with water and bring slowly to the boil. Drain and return the onions to the pan, cover with fresh water, bring to the boil and simmer until tender. Drain and reserve ½ pint (3 dl.) of the liquid.

In a mixing bowl, mix the cornflour with 3 tablespoons of the milk, to make a smooth paste.

Combine the remaining milk with the onion water and bring to the boil. Meanwhile, stir in the crumbled stock cube.

Pour the boiling liquid on to the cornflour mixture, stirring all the time, return to the pan, add the onions and continue to cook for 2 minutes, stirring constantly. Cover the surface of the sauce with greaseproof paper and cool.

**To freeze:** Pour into $\frac{1}{4}$-pint ($1\frac{1}{2}$-dl.) used cream cartons or plastic containers. Seal and freeze.

**To prepare for serving:** Immerse the container in hot water to loosen the contents. Reheat gently. *Makes $1\frac{1}{2}$ pints (scant litre).*

## Bread sauce

$1\frac{1}{2}$ pints/scant litre milk
1 small onion, peeled and finely chopped
1 blade mace
6 white peppercorns
$\frac{1}{2}$ teaspoon salt
6 oz./175 g. breadcrumbs, freshly made
2 oz./50 g. butter

Heat the milk in a saucepan and add the onion, mace and peppercorns. Simmer for 30 minutes. Strain into a clean saucepan, add the salt, breadcrumbs and butter. Simmer gently until the sauce is of a thick, creamy consistency.

**To freeze:** Cool and pack into used $\frac{1}{4}$-pint ($1\frac{1}{2}$-dl.) cream cartons or plastic containers, leaving a $\frac{1}{2}$-inch (1-cm.) headspace. Seal with a double thickness of foil.

**To prepare for serving:** Immerse the carton in hot water to loosen the contents. Turn into a small pan and reheat over gentle heat. Add 1 tablespoon cream before serving, if liked. *Makes $1\frac{1}{2}$ pints (scant litre).*

## Salmon fish cakes

3 $7\frac{1}{2}$-oz./211-g. cans salmon
$3\frac{1}{2}$ lb./$1\frac{1}{2}$ kg. potatoes, cooked and mashed
2 tablespoons chopped parsley, blanched
salt and pepper to taste
2 beaten eggs and breadcrumbs, for coating

Salmon fish cakes

Drain and flake the salmon, removing any skin and bones. Combine with the potatoes, parsley and seasoning. Divide the mixture in half and roll both pieces into sausage shapes. Cut each into 18 equal-sized pieces. Shape into cakes; dip in the beaten egg and coat with breadcrumbs.

**To freeze:** Either wrap the fish cakes in a double thickness of foil or pack in an air-tight container, with sheets of polythene tissue paper or foil between the layers. Seal and freeze.

**To prepare for serving:** Heat fat in a frying pan. Shallow-fry the required number of unthawed fish cakes. *Makes 3 servings for 4.*

10

## American fish pie

2½ lb./generous kg. fresh cod or haddock, cooked

½ pint/3 dl. white sauce, coating consistency

1 oz./25 g. parsley, blanched and chopped

salt and pepper to taste

¼ teaspoon nutmeg

juice of ½ lemon

3 lb./1¼ kg. potatoes, mashed

1 lb./450 g. tomatoes, skinned and sliced

12 oz./350 g. cheese, grated

Remove the skin and bones from the fish, flake without mashing. Add to the sauce with the parsley, seasonings and lemon juice.

**To freeze:** Arrange alternate layers of mashed potatoes and fish, with a layer of tomatoes and cheese between them, in three foil pie dishes, loaf tins or other suitable containers. Finish with layers of mashed potato. Smooth the tops and seal with a double thickness of foil.

**To prepare for serving:** Uncover the container and bake unthawed in the centre of a hot oven (400°F., 200°C., Gas Mark 6) for 40–45 minutes. Fork up the potato after the first 10 minutes of cooking time, to give a better appearance. *Makes 3 servings for 4.*

## Fish chowder

3 lb./1¼ kg. smoked haddock

bouquet garni

1 thick slice lemon

2 pints/generous litre water

1½ oz./40 g. butter

1 large onion, peeled and finely chopped

2 oz./50 g. cornflour

2 pints/generous litre milk

2 teaspoons tomato purée mixed with juice of ½ lemon

pinch pepper

¼ teaspoon ground mace

6 oz./175 g. Patna rice, boiled

Rinse the haddock and cut into large pieces. Put it into a large saucepan. Place the bouquet garni in the pan with the lemon slice and water. Bring to the boil, then lower the heat and simmer gently until the fish is cooked (approximately 15 minutes). Remove the bouquet garni and lemon slice, drain

off the liquid and set aside. Cool the fish, remove the skin and bones, then flake without mashing. Rinse the saucepan and melt the butter in it, add the onion and cook until soft but not brown. Blend the cornflour with ¼ pint (1½ dl.) of the milk; add to the pan with the remaining milk, reserved fish stock, tomato mixture, pepper and mace. Stir until boiling then reduce the heat and continue to cook for a further 2–3 minutes.

**To freeze:** Cover the liquid in the pan with a buttered paper and allow to cool. Mix in the flaked fish and rice. Pack in polythene bags, plastic or other suitable containers, leaving a ½-inch (1-cm.) headspace. Freeze.

**To prepare for serving:** Thaw, overnight, in the refrigerator. Reheat gently in a saucepan. Sprinkle each serving with chopped parsley. *Makes 3 servings for 4.*

## Beef goulash

1½ oz./40 g. lard or dripping

3½ lb./1½ kg. stewing steak, trimmed and cut into
    1-inch/2½-cm. cubes

1 clove garlic

1 teaspoon caraway seeds

1½ lb. onions, peeled and sliced

1 tablespoon paprika pepper

1 11-oz./312-g. can tomatoes

1 teaspoon sugar

salt and pepper to taste

¼ pint/1½ dl. stock or water

Heat the lard in a large saucepan. Brown the meat, a third at a time, over a brisk heat. Crush the garlic with the caraway seeds and add to the pan with the onions, lower the heat and cook until the onions are soft. Add the remaining ingredients, cover with a lid and simmer very gently for 1¼ hours.

**To freeze:** Cool rapidly and pack into foil or plastic containers, or partially freeze in a covered, foil-lined meat tin, then cut into squares and wrap each portion in a double thickness of foil. Return to the freezer.

**To prepare for serving:** Thaw at room temperature for about 4 hours. Reheat in a saucepan. Add

$\frac{1}{4}$ oz. (10 g.) beurre manié (see page 56) and cook for a further 2 minutes. Remove from the heat and add 3 tablespoons yogurt. *Makes 3 servings for 4.*

## Steak, kidney and mushrooms

3 lb./1$\frac{1}{4}$ kg. stewing steak, cut into 1-inch/2$\frac{1}{2}$-cm. cubes

12 oz./350 g. ox kidney, cored and cubed

2 oz./50 g. seasoned flour

2 oz./50 g. lard or dripping

2 large onions, peeled and sliced

12 oz./350 g. mushrooms, sliced

1$\frac{1}{2}$ pints/scant litre chicken stock or
  2 stock cubes and water

Toss the steak and kidney in the flour. Heat the fat in a frying pan. Add the onions, fry gently for 5 minutes, transfer to a casserole dish. Put the steak and kidney into the pan and fry briskly to brown. Put into the casserole dish, add the mushrooms and stock. Cover with a lid and cook in a moderate oven (350°F., 180°C., Gas Mark 4) for 1$\frac{1}{2}$ hours.

**To freeze:** Cool rapidly and pack in three foil, plastic or other suitable containers, cover and freeze.

**To prepare for serving:** Reheat without thawing in a moderate oven, or gently in a pan. *Makes 3 servings for 4.*

## Farmhouse brisket

8 oz./225 g. streaky bacon, diced

4 lb./1$\frac{3}{4}$ kg. brisket, boned and rolled

1 lb./450 g. onions, sliced

1$\frac{1}{2}$ lb./675 g. carrots, sliced

3 sticks celery, cut into $\frac{1}{2}$-inch/1-cm. pieces

1$\frac{1}{2}$ oz./40 g. plain flour

1$\frac{1}{2}$ pints/scant litre brown ale

1 tablespoon brown sugar

1 teaspoon salt

pinch pepper

1 bay leaf

Fry the bacon gently, to render down the fat. Transfer to a casserole dish. Fry the meat, briskly, in the fat, turning to brown on all sides. Put

the browned meat in the casserole with the bacon.

Lower the heat under the frying pan, add the onions and fry gently until soft but not brown. Add the carrots and celery and cook for a further 5 minutes. Stir in the flour and cook for another 2 minutes.

Spoon the vegetables around the meat and add the remaining ingredients. Cover with a lid and cook in the centre of a warm oven (325°F., 170°C., Gas Mark 3) for 2–2$\frac{1}{2}$ hours.

**To freeze:** Cool the meat and cut into slices. Pack flat in three suitable foil or plastic containers, cover closely and freeze.

**To prepare for serving:** Immerse the container in hot water to loosen the contents, transfer to a saucepan and reheat gently. *Makes 3 servings for 4.*

Braised steak with mushrooms

## Braised steak with mushrooms

2 oz./50 g. dripping or lard

3 lb./1$\frac{1}{4}$ kg. braising steak

1$\frac{1}{2}$ lb./675 g. onions, peeled and sliced

1$\frac{1}{2}$ lb./675 g. carrots, peeled and sliced

1 head celery, chopped

6 oz./175 g. mushrooms, sliced

$\frac{1}{2}$ bottle red cooking wine

1$\frac{1}{2}$ pints/scant litre beef stock or 2 stock cubes and water

salt and pepper to taste

Heat the dripping in a large pan, cut the meat into $\frac{1}{2}$-inch (1-cm.) slices and fry briskly to seal on both sides. Remove and keep hot. Add the onions, carrots, celery and mushrooms to the pan and cook for 2 minutes. Put the vegetables and meat into the casserole. Add the wine, stock and seasoning. Cover and cook in a moderately hot oven (375°F., 190°C., Gas Mark 5) for 1½ hours.

**To freeze:** Cool rapidly. Pack in three foil or plastic containers or in polythene bags. Seal and freeze.

**To prepare for serving:** Remove from freezer 2 hours before use. Heat in a moderately hot oven (375°F., 190°C., Gas Mark 5) for 35–40 minutes. *Makes 3 servings for 4.*

Portuguese cobbler

## Portuguese cobbler

2 oz./50 g. dripping or lard

2 large onions, peeled and chopped

2½ lb./generous kg. pie veal, cut into 2-inch/5-cm. cubes

2 oz./50 g. flour

2 15-oz./425-g. cans tomato soup

1 lb./450 g. carrots, peeled and sliced

salt and pepper

2 green peppers, de-seeded and diced

6 oz./175 g. mushrooms, sliced

*For the topping:*

12 oz./350 g. plain flour

1½ teaspoons baking powder

1 teaspoon salt

4 oz./100 g. margarine or lard

¼ pint plus 2–3 tablespoons/1½ dl. milk

Melt the fat in a 4-pint (2-litre) flameproof dish, fry the onions and meat until lightly browned, remove them from the dish. Stir the flour into the fat, add the soup and bring to the boil. Return the onions and meat to the dish, add the carrots

and season to taste. Cook in a slow oven (300°F., 150°C., Gas Mark 2) for 2 hours. Add the green peppers and mushrooms 20 minutes before the end of the cooking time. Remove from the oven and turn the thermostat up to 425°F., 220°C., Gas Mark 7. Sieve the flour, baking powder and salt into a mixing bowl. Rub in the fat and add sufficient milk to make a soft dough. Cut into 1½–2-inch (4–5-cm.) circles, place on a greased baking sheet and brush with milk. Bake in the top of the pre-heated oven for 10–12 minutes. Cool on a wire rack.

**To freeze:** Cool the meat mixture and pack in three foil pie dishes. Seal with double thicknesses of foil. Pack cobblers separately in polythene bags. Seal tightly and freeze.

**To prepare for serving:** Place unthawed meat in a pre-heated oven (325°F., 170°C., Gas Mark 3) for about 1 hour. 10 minutes before the end of cooking time, remove the foil and arrange the cobblers to cover the surface of the meat. *Makes 3 servings for 4.*

## Osso buco

6 lb./2¾ kg. shin of veal, chopped in 2-inch/5-cm. pieces

2 oz./50 g. seasoned flour

4 oz./100 g. butter or margarine

2 carrots, peeled and cut into thick slices

1 onion, peeled and sliced

1 clove garlic

1 teaspoon salt

1 2¼-oz./64-g. can tomato purée

¾ pint/4 dl. chicken stock or 1 stock cube and water

pinch pepper

1 bay leaf

1 teaspoon sugar

Coat the veal with seasoned flour. Melt the butter in a large frying pan and put the carrot and onion into the pan. Peel the garlic, crush with the salt and add it to the vegetables in the pan. Fry gently for 5 minutes. Transfer the vegetables to a large saucepan. Put the veal into the frying pan and brown on all sides, over strong heat. Transfer the meat to the saucepan and add the remaining ingredients. Cover with a lid and simmer gently for 2 hours. Strain the sauce and reserve.

**To freeze:** Cool, discard the vegetables and bay leaf. Remove the meat from the bones. Pack the veal into three plastic, foil or other suitable containers. Divide the sauce between the three servings. Seal and freeze.

**To prepare for serving:** Immerse the container in hot water to loosen the contents. Reheat in a covered saucepan over gentle heat. *Makes 3 servings for 4.*

Country braise

## Country braise

2 oz./50 g. lard or dripping

2 large onions, peeled and sliced

1 lb./450 g. carrots, peeled and sliced

1 large cooking apple, peeled, cored and sliced

3 lb./1¼ kg. stewing veal, cut into 1-inch/2½-cm. cubes

2 oz./50 g. seasoned flour

¾ pint/4 dl. chicken stock or 1 stock cube and water

3 tablespoons tomato ketchup

4 oz./100 g. prunes, soaked for 2 hours and stoned

2 oz./50 g. almonds, blanched and chopped

Heat the lard in a large saucepan, add the onions, carrots and apples and fry until lightly browned; remove from the pan. Toss the veal in the flour and fry gently for 5 minutes. Return the vegetables to the saucepan, add the stock and tomato ketchup, bring to the boil then simmer very gently for 1 hour.

**To freeze:** Cool, add the prunes and almonds. Pack in three plastic containers or polythene bags, seal and freeze.

**To prepare for serving:** Thaw at room temperature, allowing approximately 4 hours. Turn into a saucepan, bring to the boil, cover with a lid and simmer for 30 minutes. *Makes 3 servings for 4.*

## Devilled rabbit

12 rabbit pieces

2 tablespoons malt vinegar

2 tablespoons mild mustard, freshly made

1 tablespoon curry powder

5 tablespoons corn oil

12 oz./350 g. pickled pork, diced

2 onions, peeled and chopped

seasoned flour, for coating

1½ pints/scant litre chicken stock or
    2 stock cubes and water

4 tablespoons cornflour

6 tablespoons milk

salt and pepper to taste

1 teaspoon white vinegar

Put the rabbit pieces into a bowl of cold water, add 2 tablespoons vinegar and leave to soak for about 1 hour. Drain and pat dry. Mix the mustard and curry powder. Spread over the rabbit joints. Leave for another 30–40 minutes for the flavour to penetrate. Heat the oil in a heavy pan. Add the pork and onion. Cook the onion until transparent but not brown. Dip the rabbit pieces into the flour; add them to the pan and brown lightly on all sides. Pour the stock over and stir until boiling. Cover with a lid and simmer gently for 1 hour. Blend the cornflour with the milk and add to the pan. Remove from the heat, check the seasoning and add the white vinegar. Cool.

**To freeze:** Pack into three foil-lined serving dishes. Cover with foil and partially freeze. Remove from the serving dishes, when sufficiently solid to do so, and over-wrap with double or heavy duty foil. Seal and freeze.

**To prepare for serving:** Unwrap and return to the original dish. Reheat in a hot oven (400°F., 200°C., Gas Mark 6). *Makes 3 servings for 4.*

## Liver and onion casserole

3 lb./1¼ kg. ox liver, sliced and trimmed
2 oz./50 g. seasoned flour
3 oz./75 g. dripping or lard
2 lb./900 g. onions, peeled and sliced
¾ pint/4 dl. beef stock or 1 stock cube and water
½ teaspoon mixed herbs

Soak the liver in cold, salted water for 30 minutes. Dry on absorbent paper then coat in the seasoned flour. Melt the fat in a heavy saucepan or flame-proof casserole and cook the onion gently until soft but not brown. Remove the onion and set aside. Fry the liver briskly in the remaining fat to seal on both sides. Return the onion to the pan and add any remaining seasoned flour. Stir well, then add the stock and herbs. Cover the casserole with a lid and cook in a warm oven (325°F., 170°C., Gas Mark 3) for 1½ hours.

**To freeze:** Cool rapidly. Spoon into three plastic or foil containers. Seal and freeze.

**To prepare for serving:** Thaw overnight in the refrigerator. Reheat gently, in a covered pan. *Makes 3 servings for 4.*

## Cutlet turnovers

12 large lamb cutlets, boned
1½ lb./675 g. puff pastry
½ pint/3 dl. onion sauce (see page 9)

Trim the fat from the meat and roll tightly. Secure each with a cocktail stick. Grill and set aside to cool. Remove the cocktail sticks.

For ease of handling, cut the pastry into three equal pieces. Roll each piece into a 16-inch (40-cm.) square, trim the edges and cut into quarters. Spoon a little sauce into the centre of each square and top with a lamb cutlet. Damp two adjoining edges of each square and fold over to make a triangle. Seal and pinch the edges. Place in the refrigerator to chill the pastry thoroughly.

**To freeze:** Pack upright, in a suitable polythene container, with foil or polythene tissue dividing papers between each. Seal and freeze.

**To prepare for serving:** Place, unthawed, on a wet baking sheet. Brush with milk, cook in a very hot oven (450°F., 230°C., Gas Mark 8) for 20 minutes. *Makes 12.*

Moussaka

## Moussaka

2 oz./50 g. lard or dripping
1 large onion, peeled and finely chopped
3 lb./1¼ kg. raw shoulder lamb, minced
salt and pepper to taste
3 tablespoons tomato purée
1 tablespoon sugar
3 large aubergines, sliced and sprinkled with salt
1 clove garlic, crushed
1 11-oz./312-g. can tomatoes
¾ pint/4 dl. cheese sauce
3 oz./75 g. cheese, grated

Heat 1 oz. (25 g.) of the lard or dripping in a saucepan. Add the onion and allow to colour. Add the meat and stir over a brisk heat to brown. Season with salt and pepper, add the tomato purée and sugar. Set aside. Wash the aubergines under cold, running water. Dry on kitchen paper. Heat the remaining fat in the pan, add 2 aubergines to the pan and cook for 5–7 minutes, add the garlic and tomatoes. Cover the pan and continue to cook for a further 5 minutes.

**To freeze:** Divide the meat mixture between three foil dishes. Cover with the aubergine and tomato mixture. Top with the cheese sauce and remaining aubergine slices. Sprinkle 1 oz. (25 g.) cheese on each dish. Seal with double thicknesses of foil and freeze.

**To prepare for serving:** Uncover, place in a hot oven (400°F., 200°C., Gas Mark 6) for 40 minutes. *Makes 3 servings for 4.*

15

## Potted hough

1½ lb./675 g. shin of beef
2–2½ lb./about 1 kg. knuckle of veal, chopped by the
  butcher
1½ teaspoons salt
6 peppercorns
1 bay leaf

Put the beef, veal and salt into a large saucepan, add enough water to cover and bring to the boil. Simmer until the meat is tender (approximately 3 hours). Strain the liquid into a clean saucepan. Cool the meat, cut into small pieces and divide between three 1-pint (6-dl.) foil pudding basins.

Put the bones into the stock with the peppercorns and bay leaf. Boil rapidly, without a lid, to reduce to ½ pint (3 dl.). Strain the stock on to the meat and leave to set.

**To freeze:** Cover the basins with double or heavy duty foil, seal and freeze.

**To prepare for serving:** Thaw overnight in the refrigerator. Serve with salad.   *Makes 3 servings for 4.*

## Terrine of game

2 oz./50 g. butter
1 pheasant, plucked and drawn
2 partridges, plucked and drawn
12 oz./350 g. shin of veal, chopped into 2-inch/5-cm.
  pieces
3 pints/1¾ litres stock or water
3 cloves
10 white peppercorns
2 teaspoons salt
¼ pint/1½ dl. dry white wine

Melt the butter in a large, heavy saucepan. Brown the birds over a brisk heat. Put all the birds back into the pan with the veal, stock, cloves, peppercorns and salt. Bring to the boil; lower the heat, cover and simmer for 1½–2 hours. Remove the birds and the veal from the pan, cool and cut into pieces. Discard the bones. Strain the stock into a clean saucepan, add the wine and boil rapidly to reduce by two-thirds. Meanwhile, arrange the game in three foil-lined terrines or small pie dishes. Skim the fat from the stock and pour it over the game. (Older birds may be used for this dish.)

**To freeze:** Cool rapidly, until set. Cover with foil and partially freeze. Remove from the terrine and over-wrap with a double or heavy duty foil. Return to the freezer.

**To prepare for serving:** Thaw overnight in the refrigerator. Serve in the original dish.   *Makes 3 servings for 4.*

## Beef galantine

2 lb./900 g. rump steak
12 oz./350 g. cooked ham
1 large onion, peeled and quartered
1½ lb./675 g. tomatoes, skinned
6 oz./175 g. white breadcrumbs
2 eggs, lightly beaten
salt and pepper to taste

Cut away any fat or gristle from the steak and ham. Mince the steak, ham and onion finely, by passing it through the mincer two or three times. Blend or sieve the tomatoes and add to the meat mixture with the remaining ingredients. Mix thoroughly to combine.

Divide the mixture into three equal portions. Press each into a 1-pint (6-dl.) foil basin. Cover with aluminium foil and steam gently for 3 hours.

Cool in the refrigerator or larder with a kitchen weight on each basin.

**To freeze:** When quite cold, re-cover the dishes with foil and seal before freezing.

**To prepare for serving:** Thaw overnight in the refrigerator or at room temperature for 4 hours. *Makes 3 servings for 4.*

## Cornish pasties

1½ lb./675 g. shortcrust pastry
*For the filling:*
1¼ lb./550 g. lean beefsteak
2 medium potatoes, diced
2 medium onions, peeled and finely chopped
2 tablespoons chopped, blanched parsley
salt and pepper to taste
1 tablespoon stock or water

Mince the meat finely and add to the other filling ingredients. Divide the pastry into 12 portions and roll each piece into a 5-inch (13-cm.) circle. Put a spoonful of the filling into the centre of each piece of pastry, damp the edges, fold in half and seal. Flute the edges by pinching between the thumb and first two fingers. Stand the pastries upright on a greased baking sheet, brush with egg and milk and set aside in a cool place for 30 minutes, to allow the pastry to relax. Bake in the centre of a moderately hot oven (375°F., 190°C., Gas Mark 5) for 35 minutes.

**To freeze:** Allow to become completely cold. Pack in plastic, aluminium foil or other suitable containers, seal and freeze.

**To prepare for serving:** Allow to thaw at room temperature for approximately 4 hours. Reheat in a cool oven. *Makes 3 servings for 4.*

## Devonshire pasties

1 lb./450 g. shortcrust pastry
*For the filling:*
1 lb./450 g. raw beef, minced
12 oz./350 g. mushrooms, chopped
1 11-oz./312-g. can sweetcorn with peppers
salt and pepper
beaten egg

Mix the minced meat, mushrooms and drained sweetcorn and season with salt and pepper. Roll out the pastry to about $\frac{1}{8}$ inch (3 mm.) thick and cut into circles around a saucer. Divide the filling evenly between the pasties, damp the edges with water, fold over and seal. Brush with beaten egg and make a couple of slashes on top of each pasty. Bake in a hot oven (425°F., 220°C., Gas Mark 7) for about 30 minutes, when the pastry should be crisp and golden.

**To freeze:** Allow to become completely cold. Pack into a suitable container, cover closely and freeze.

**To prepare for serving:** Reheat frozen pasties in a moderate oven (350°F., 180°C., Gas Mark 4) for approximately 20 minutes. *Makes 3 servings for 4.*

## Chicken special

2 medium-sized chickens
3 pints/1 $\frac{3}{4}$ litres water
1 lb./450 g. streaky bacon
1 lb./450 g. button mushrooms
3 oz./75 g. butter
3 oz./75 g. flour
salt and pepper to taste

Simmer the chickens in the water until tender. Set aside until cool. Reserve the stock for the sauce. Chop the bacon into 2-inch (5-cm.) pieces after removing the rind. Cut the mushrooms in half. Fry the bacon until crisp and remove from the pan. Cook the mushrooms gently in the bacon fat. Melt the butter in a clean saucepan, add the flour and cook for 1 minute. Season to taste, remove from the heat and gradually stir in 1$\frac{1}{2}$ pints (scant litre) stock. Return to the heat and bring to the boil, stirring. Remove all the flesh from the chickens and cut into bite-size pieces; add to the sauce with the bacon and mushrooms.

**To freeze:** Cool rapidly, pack in foil, plastic or other suitable containers. Seal tightly and freeze.

**To prepare for serving:** Immerse the container in hot water to loosen the contents. Turn into a saucepan and reheat gently. Add a small packet of frozen peas and continue to cook for a further 7 minutes. *Makes 3 servings for 4.*

## Creamed pimento chicken pie

6 oz./175 g. butter
5 oz./150 g. flour
salt and pepper to taste
2 pints/generous litre chicken stock or
    2 stock cubes and water
1 pint/6 dl. milk
2$\frac{1}{2}$ lb./generous kg. cooked chicken, chopped
1 small can pimento
*For the pastry crust:*
1 lb./450 g. flaky pastry

Melt the butter over low heat, blend in the flour smoothly and add the seasonings. Gradually stir in the chicken stock and the milk. Bring to the boil, stirring constantly, allow to boil for 1 minute. Stir in the chicken, and the finely chopped pimento together with the liquid from the can. Cool and pack into three foil pie dishes.

To make the crust, divide the pastry into three, roll out thinly and use to cover the pies. Damp the edges and decorate without breaking the seal. Pierce a hole in the centre and bake in a hot oven (425°F., 220°C., Gas Mark 7) for 15 minutes. If necessary, reduce the heat slightly and continue cooking for another 5–10 minutes or until golden brown.

**To freeze:** Wrap each pie separately in double or heavy duty foil. Seal tightly and freeze.

**To prepare for serving:** Thaw in the refrigerator and reheat in a moderately hot oven (375°F., 190°C., Gas Mark 5) for about 1 hour.

**Note:** The pies can be frozen with the pastry unbaked, after sealing the edges of the crusts. Do not pierce a hole in the pastry. Place unbaked in the freezer to harden the pastry, then wrap in foil. Freeze. *Makes 3 servings for 4.*

## Scalloped turkey with rice

8 oz./225 g. Patna rice

3 oz./75 g. butter or margarine

1 lb./450 g. mushrooms

3 oz./75 g. flour

salt and pepper to taste

$\frac{3}{4}$ pint/4 dl. hot milk

1 pint/6 dl. hot chicken stock

$2\frac{1}{2}$ lb./generous kg. cooked turkey, chopped

1 medium green pepper, de-seeded

Cook the rice in plenty of boiling salted water until just tender. Drain and rinse in a colander, using fresh, hot water. Melt 1 oz. (25 g.) of the butter and fry the mushrooms for 1 minute only. Remove from the pan, add the rest of the butter and make a thick sauce with the flour, seasoning, milk and stock. Stir constantly over moderate heat until the sauce is smooth and thick.

**To freeze:** Pack in foil dishes or other suitable containers, with layers of rice, mushrooms and turkey. Pour one-third of the sauce into each container. Chop the pepper finely and sprinkle evenly over the three containers. Cool quickly. Cover closely with foil.

**To prepare for serving:** Put into the top of a moderately hot oven (375°F., 190°C., Gas Mark 5), turning frequently to heat right through. *Makes 3 servings for 4.*

Cider gammon with apples

## Cider gammon with apples

12 slices gammon

black pepper to taste

6 oz./175 g. butter

1$\frac{1}{2}$ pints/scant litre cider

12 oz./350 g. button onions

8 sticks celery

9 tomatoes, quartered

12 oz./350 g. mushrooms

6 dessert apples, cored and sliced

3 oz./75 g. flour

Place the gammon in a casserole, sprinkle in the pepper. Add half the butter and 2 tablespoons of the cider. Cover with a lid and bake in a moderately hot oven (375°F., 190°C., Gas Mark 5) for 15–20 minutes. Meanwhile melt the remaining butter and fry all the vegetables and the apples in it. Add the flour and cook, stirring, for a few minutes. Gradually pour in the cider, and stir until smooth. Pour over the gammon, re-cover the casserole and continue cooking in the oven for a further 20 minutes.

**To freeze:** Cool rapidly, put into three suitable containers, cover closely and seal before freezing.

**To prepare for serving:** Thaw at room temperature for about 6 hours. Reheat in a covered casserole in a moderately hot oven. Stir in $\frac{1}{4}$ pint (1$\frac{1}{2}$ dl.) single cream just before serving. *Makes 3 servings for 4.*

# Steak and kidney pudding

*For the pastry:*

1 lb./450 g. self-raising flour

2 teaspoons salt

pinch pepper

8 oz./225 g. shredded beef suet

cold water to mix

*For the filling:*

2 lb./900 g. stewing steak, cut in 1-inch/2½-cm. cubes

8 oz./225 g. ox kidney, cored and cut in pieces

1 oz./25 g. seasoned flour

6 tablespoons water

Sift together the flour and salt. Add the suet and enough water to make a firm dough. Cut off one-third of the pastry and divide the remaining pastry into three. Use these pieces to line three 1½-pint (1-litre) greased foil pudding basins.

Toss the meat in the seasoned flour and divide between the basins. Pour 2 tablespoons water into each basin. Damp the edges of the pastry and top the basins with the remaining pastry, rolled into circles. Cover with greased foil and steam for 3 hours.

**To freeze:** Cool quickly. Put into a polythene bag. Seal and freeze.

**To prepare for serving:** Remove the polythene bag and thaw at room temperature for 6–8 hours. Steam for 1½ hours. *Makes 3 servings for 4.*

### Variations

**Rabbit and bacon pudding:** Omit the steak and kidney and use 2 lb. (900 g.) jointed rabbit, blanched, 1 lb. (450 g.) lean collar bacon, soaked and cut in cubes, 2 large onions, sliced, 4 oz. (100 g.) mushrooms, chopped, 2 cooking apples, peeled, cored and chopped and 1 teaspoon sage.

**Veal, gammon and mushroom pudding:** Omit the steak and kidney and use 2 lb. (900 g.) pie veal, cut in 1-inch (2½-cm.) cubes, 12 oz. (350 g.) lean gammon, cut into ½-inch (1-cm.) pieces, 8 oz. (225 g.) mushrooms, chopped, grated rind of 1 lemon and ¼ teaspoon dried thyme.

**Rhubarb and orange pudding:** Omit the steak, kidney, flour and water and use 2 lb. (900 g.) rhubarb, cut in 1-inch (2½-cm.) pieces, the grated rind and chopped segments of 2 large oranges and 6–8 oz. (175–225 g.) sugar. Steam for 2 hours only before freezing.

**Gooseberry pudding:** Omit the steak, kidney, flour and water and use 2 lb. (900 g.) gooseberries, topped and tailed, and 6–8 oz. (175–225 g.) sugar. Steam for 2 hours only before freezing.

**Plum and apple pudding:** Omit the steak, kidney, flour and water, and use 2 lb. (900 g.) plums, halved and stoned, 2 cooking apples, peeled, cored and sliced and 8 oz. (225 g.) sugar. Steam for 2 hours only before freezing.

# Apricot oat crumble

1 lb./450 g. dried apricots, soaked and stewed

2 oz./50 g. plain flour

4 oz./100 g. butter, melted

6 oz./175 g. demerara sugar

8 oz./225 g. rolled oats

Divide the fruit into three portions and spread into the bases of three 1-pint (6-dl.) foil dishes. Mix the flour, butter and sugar into the rolled oats and scatter over the top of the fruit.

**To freeze:** Seal with a double thickness of foil and freeze.

**To prepare for serving:** Remove the cover and sprinkle the surface of the crumble with sugar. Bake in a moderate oven (350°F., 180°C., Gas Mark 4), without thawing, for 40 minutes. *Makes 3 servings for 4.*

# Traditional trifle

8 individual sponge cakes, crumbled

6 tablespoons sherry

6 tablespoons raspberry jam

12 macaroons

2 oz./50 g. flaked almonds

¾ pint/4 dl. cold custard

Divide the cake crumbs and press into the bases of 12 individual foil pie plates. Sprinkle with sherry and top with raspberry jam. Sprinkle with crumbled macaroons and flaked almonds, and top with custard.

**To freeze:** Seal the dishes with foil and freeze.

**To prepare for serving:** Thaw, covered, at room temperature for about 2 hours. Decorate with whipped cream. *Makes 3 servings for 4.*

## Steamed syrup pudding

3 tablespoons golden syrup
12 oz./350 g. self-raising flour
4 teaspoons baking powder
1 teaspoon mixed spice
½ teaspoon salt
8 oz./225 g. luxury margarine
8 oz./225 g. castor sugar
4 large eggs
3 tablespoons milk

Put a tablespoon of syrup into each of three 1-pint (6-dl.) foil pudding basins. Sieve the flour, baking powder, mixed spice and salt into a mixing bowl. Add the remaining ingredients, beat for 2 minutes or until all the ingredients are blended. Spoon equal quantities of the mixture into the pudding basins. Seal the tops of the basins with foil and steam for 1½ hours.

**To freeze:** Cool, re-seal with double or heavy duty foil.

**To prepare for serving:** Steam the pudding for approximately 30 minutes, or until hot. *Makes 3 servings for 4.*

## Perth pudding and honey sauce

6 oz./175 g. butter
6 oz./175 g. castor sugar
3 eggs
9 oz./250 g. self-raising flour
3 oz./75 g. currants
4½ oz./125 g. sultanas
about 3 tablespoons milk

Cream together the butter and sugar until light and fluffy. Lightly beat the eggs and gradually add to the creamed mixture, beating well. Add a little flour with the egg if the mixture shows signs of curdling. Fold in the remaining flour and the dried fruit. Well grease three 1-pint (6-dl.) pudding basins and two-thirds fill with the mixture. Cover the basins with well-greased double

Perth pudding and honey sauce

or heavy duty foil and crimp tightly under the edges of the basins to seal. Ensure that the water in the steamer or saucepan is boiling, put in the puddings and steam for 1–1½ hours. Remove from the steamer and allow to cool completely.

**To freeze:** Check seal of foil all around edges. Label and freeze.

**To prepare for serving:** Get a steamer or saucepan of water boiling, place the frozen pudding in the prepared pan and steam for 40 minutes. To make the sauce, melt together 4 oz. (100 g.) butter and 4 tablespoons clear honey and serve warm with the pudding. *Makes 3 servings for 4.*

Peel, halve and core the pears and place at once in warm syrup.

Arrange the pears carefully in rigid containers, leaving a good headspace, and fill with sufficient syrup to cover.

Place crumpled foil over the pears to keep them submerged.

Pears in spiced honey syrup are delicious served with whipped cream and cinnamon.

## Pears in spiced honey syrup

6 oz./175 g. clear honey
1½ pints/scant litre water
3 oz./75 g. crystallised ginger, sliced
good pinch cinnamon
6 tablespoons lemon juice
3 lb./1¼ kg. dessert pears, not quite ripe

Use a wide shallow pan which will allow the pears to lie in a single layer or cook the pears a few at a time. Put the honey and water in the pan and stir over a gentle heat until the honey dissolves. Add the sliced ginger, cinnamon and lemon juice. Peel and halve the pears. Remove the cores and put the fruit immediately into the syrup. The pears must be kept covered with syrup throughout cooking and freezing to avoid discoloration. Poach them gently until they are tender.

**To freeze:** Stand the pan in cold water to cool them quickly. Arrange pears carefully in plastic containers leaving a ¾-inch (1½-cm.) headspace, cover with syrup, then place crumpled foil on top of the fruit to keep submerged. Cover, freeze.

**To prepare for serving:** Thaw at room temperature and serve while the fruit is still chilled. Decorate with piped whipped cream and a sprinkling of cinnamon. *Makes 3 servings for 4.*

## Raisin ice cream

1 14-oz./396-g. and 1 6-oz./170-g. can evaporated milk, chilled
3 oz./75 g. castor sugar
juice of 2 lemons
6 oz./175 g. seedless raisins
½ teaspoon vanilla essence
1 tablespoon gelatine
3 tablespoons warm water

Whisk all the evaporated milk until thick. Beat in the sugar, lemon juice, raisins and vanilla essence. Dissolve the gelatine in water in a small saucepan. Heat gently, but do not allow to boil.

Quickly stir into the evaporated milk and whisk until on the point of setting. Pour into a plastic container, cover with a lid and freeze for 2 hours. Whisk the mixture to break down the ice particles, cover and freeze again. *Makes 3 servings for 4.*

## Butterscotch sauce

6 tablespoons golden syrup
2 oz./50 g. brown sugar
1 oz./25 g. butter
$\frac{3}{4}$ pint/4 dl. water
1 tablespoon custard powder, mixed with
  juice of 1 $\frac{1}{2}$ lemons

Melt the syrup, brown sugar and butter in a heavy saucepan, heat gently to combine. Remove from the heat and add the water, pour over the custard mixture and return to the saucepan. Stir over gentle heat until thickened.

**To freeze:** Cool and pack into boiling bags or plastic containers. Seal and freeze.

**To prepare for serving:** Immerse the bag in boiling water for 10 minutes. Immerse plastic containers in hot water for 15 minutes. Serve hot with ice cream or other desserts. *Makes $\frac{3}{4}$ pint (4 dl.).*

Sauces for ice cream

## Raspberry sauce

1 lb./450 g. raspberry jam
juice of 2 lemons
$\frac{1}{2}$ pint/3 dl. water
2 tablespoons arrowroot

Combine the jam, lemon juice and water in a saucepan. Blend the arrowroot with some of the liquid, bring the remainder to the boil and add the blended arrowroot. Cook for a further 2 minutes stirring constantly. Strain to remove the pips.

**To freeze:** Cool and pack into boiling bags or plastic containers. Seal and freeze.

**To prepare for serving:** Immerse the bag in boiling water for 10 minutes. Immerse plastic containers in hot water for 15 minutes. Serve hot with ice cream or other desserts. *Makes 1 pint (6 dl.).*

## Dark chocolate sauce

1 lb./450 g. plain chocolate
$\frac{1}{4}$ pint/1 $\frac{1}{2}$ dl. clear honey
$\frac{1}{4}$ pint/1 $\frac{1}{2}$ dl. lemon juice
4 tablespoons cornflour
1 pint/6 dl. water
8 oz./225 g. unsalted butter

Place all the ingredients in a saucepan and heat gently until the chocolate has melted. Stir briskly until the mixture comes to the boil and is smooth and thick. Remove from the heat and cool, stirring frequently.

**To freeze:** Cool and pack into boiling bags or plastic containers. Seal and freeze.

**To prepare for serving:** Immerse the bag in boiling water for 10 minutes. Immerse plastic containers in hot water for 15 minutes. Serve hot with ice cream or other desserts. *Makes 2 pints (generous litre).*

# White bread

*Dry mix:*
1 lb./450 g. plain flour
2 teaspoons salt
$\frac{1}{2}$ oz./15 g. lard
*Yeast liquid:*
$\frac{1}{2}$ oz./15 g. fresh yeast and $\frac{1}{2}$ pint/3 dl. water, or
  2 teaspoons dried yeast, 1 teaspoon sugar and
  $\frac{1}{2}$ pint/3 dl. tepid water (110°F., 43°C.)

Mix the fresh yeast with the water, or dissolve the sugar in the water and sprinkle over the dried yeast. Leave until frothy, about 10 minutes. Sift the flour with the salt and rub in the lard. Mix the dry ingredients with the yeast liquid using a wooden fork or spoon, then work with one hand to a firm dough, adding extra flour, if needed, until the dough leaves the sides of the bowl clean. Turn on to a lightly floured board and knead thoroughly to stretch and develop the dough. To do this fold the dough towards you, then push down and away with the palm of the hand. Repeat for about 10 minutes until the dough feels firm and elastic and no longer sticky. After kneading, shape the dough into a ball. Place in a large, lightly greased polythene bag.

**To freeze unrisen dough:** Seal the bag tightly and place in the freezer. If the dough might rise slightly before freezing, leave a 1-inch (2$\frac{1}{2}$-cm.) space above the dough.

**To freeze risen dough:** Loosely tie the bag, leaving room for the dough to rise. Allow to rise until double in size:
Quick rise: 45–60 minutes in a warm place.

Slower rise: 2 hours at average room temperature. Overnight rise: up to 12 hours in a cold larder or refrigerator.

Risen dough springs back when pressed with a lightly floured finger. Turn the risen dough on to a lightly floured board and flatten firmly with the knuckles to knock out air bubbles, then knead until firm. Place in a lightly greased polythene bag, tightly seal and place in the freezer.

**To prepare unrisen dough for use:** Thaw for about 5–6 hours at room temperature, then leave to rise and knock back, as above.

**To prepare risen dough for use:** Thaw for about 5–6 hours at room temperature.

**To shape the dough:** For tin loaves, divide the dough into the quantity required (i.e., leave whole for a large loaf, or divide into two for two small loaves) and shape the loaves as follows. Flatten the dough with the knuckles to an oblong the width of the tin. Fold in three and turn over so that the seam is underneath. Smooth over the top and tuck in the ends. The loaves are now ready to rise again (this is known as proving). Put the tins inside a greased polythene bag and leave until the dough rises to the tops of the tins. This takes 30–40 minutes at room temperature, or leave in a refrigerator if a slow rising is more convenient. Remove from the polythene bag and bake the loaves in the centre of a very hot oven (450°F., 230°C., Gas Mark 8) for 30–40 minutes or until the loaves shrink slightly from the sides of the tins and sound hollow when tapped on the base; cool on a wire tray.

# Chapter Two

# Chain cooking

Planning ahead can save you a great deal of time and effort, as well as money. We've seen how this applies to cooking main dishes in large quantities, so that you can serve one meal at once, and freeze the rest. But if the freezer is used really intelligently, this kind of planning can be carried even further.

At the time of year when a seasonal glut makes apples cheap, for instance, buy a really large quantity. One afternoon's work in the kitchen will keep you supplied for many months to come with apple purée for pies and other sweets, apple sauce for meat dishes, fresh sliced apples for cooking as well as using in salads, when this most popular of all fruits is scarce and expensive.

You may notice a special offer of chicken at a lower-than-usual price, either by your usual frozen food supplier, or at a local supermarket. Sometimes one shop brings down the price of chicken to a level that is not really economic, but which tempts many extra customers to do a week's shopping for groceries there, instead of at their usual stores. When chicken is a 'loss leader', as it's called, rush in and take advantage of the bargain. This is the time to go in for chain cooking. Buy a dozen roasters, and a few hours work will provide you with plenty of frozen pieces ready to cook, various prepared chicken dishes that only need thawing and reheating, and lots of good strong stock made from the carcasses.

It may be that you just happen to have some time to spare. No food is specially cheap, but you do have free time and stove space for a big cook-up. A large quantity of minced beef, always a good economy buy for main meal dishes, can be made up into a variety of dishes and sauces. Again, a few hours spent cooking ahead will save you many chores in the months to come.

Minced meat can be shaped into patties and packed in plastic containers with foil or polythene tissue paper dividers. Pat out on a floured board to about ½-inch (1-cm.) thickness and trim to fit the container. Transfer with a fish slice to the container.

## MINCED BEEF CHAIN

Make up 7 lb. (3 kg.) of the basic recipe, then by making simple additions you can produce five different dishes – amounting to 40 servings.

### Basic meat recipe

2 oz./50 g. dripping or lard

2 lb./900 g. onions, peeled and chopped

3 cloves garlic, crushed

7 lb./3 kg. minced beef

1 2¼-oz./64-g. can tomato purée

2 tablespoons sugar

2 teaspoons salt

½ teaspoon pepper

Heat the fat in a very large saucepan or a preserving pan, then fry the onion and garlic over gentle heat until soft but not brown. Add the meat and fry briskly, stirring constantly to brown. Mix in the remaining ingredients and remove from the heat.

## Steak maison

2 lb./900 g. basic meat recipe

2 green peppers, de-seeded and chopped

4 tablespoons tomato ketchup

1 teaspoon salt

2 16-oz./454-g. cans baked beans in tomato sauce

Combine the meat, peppers, ketchup and salt in a saucepan. Cover with a lid and simmer over a low heat for 30 minutes. Add the baked beans.

**To freeze:** Cool rapidly. Line a meat tin with aluminium foil. Pour the mixture into the tin, cover with foil then partially freeze. Remove from the tin and cut into portions. Quickly re-wrap in double or heavy duty foil and return to the freezer.

**To prepare for serving:** Unwrap the required number of portions. Reheat in a casserole in the oven or in a tightly covered saucepan. *Makes 2 servings for 4.*

## Baboti

1 slice bread, 1½ inches/3½ cm. thick

½ pint/3 dl. milk

2 lb./900 g. basic meat recipe

1 tablespoon Worcestershire sauce

3 tablespoons curry powder

Trim the crusts from the bread, cut into cubes and soak in the milk for 10 minutes. Mix with meat, Worcestershire sauce and curry powder.

**To freeze:** Pack into foil dishes without pressing the mixture down. Seal with double or heavy duty foil and freeze.

**To prepare for serving:** Thaw in the refrigerator overnight. Uncover and pour a lightly whisked egg over the meat. Cook in a moderate oven (350°F., 180°C., Gas Mark 4) for approximately 40 minutes. *Makes 2 servings for 4.*

## Chilli con carne

1½–2 lb./675–900 g. basic meat recipe

2 teaspoons chilli powder

2 16-oz./454-g. cans baked beans

1 11-oz./312-g. can tomatoes

Combine all the ingredients in a saucepan. Cover with a lid and simmer gently for 40 minutes.

**To freeze and prepare for serving:** Follow the method of Steak maison. *Makes 2 servings for 4.*

## Shepherd's pie

2 lb./900 g. basic meat recipe

1 tablespoon curry powder

2 oz./50 g. flour

2 tablespoons brown table sauce

¾ pint/4 dl. stock or 1 stock cube and water

3 lb./1¼ kg. mashed potato

salt and pepper to taste

Put the meat into a saucepan and stir in the curry powder, flour and sauce. Cook over gentle heat, stirring constantly, for 5 minutes. Add the stock, bring to the boil and cover with a tight-fitting lid. Simmer gently for 20 minutes.

**To freeze:** Cool rapidly. Fill aluminium pie dishes or loaf tins two-thirds full. Cover with lightly seasoned mashed potato. Then smooth the tops and seal with double foil and freeze.

**To prepare for serving:** Remove the foil cover. Reheat in the top of a fairly hot oven (400°F., 200°C., Gas Mark 6) for 30–40 minutes. Remember to fork up the potato after the first 10 minutes of cooking. *Makes 2 servings for 4.*

## Bolognaise sauce

1 lb./450 g. basic meat recipe

1 11-oz./312-g. can tomatoes

¾ pint/4 dl. stock or 1 stock cube and water

¼ pint/1½ dl. red cooking wine (optional)

Combine all the ingredients in a pan. Cover with a tight-fitting lid, simmer gently for about 1 hour.

**To freeze:** Cool rapidly. Pour into used cream cartons or plastic containers, leaving a ½-inch (1-cm.) headspace. Seal and freeze.

**To prepare for serving:** Immerse the container in hot water for a few minutes, to loosen the sauce. Turn into a saucepan, cover with a lid and bring to boiling point. *Makes 2 servings for 4.*

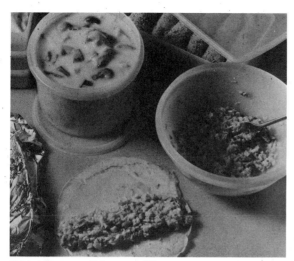

Chicken turnovers, Vol-au-vent filling, Kromeskies and Chicken pancakes

Chicken pieces, plain and coated

## CHICKEN CHAIN

The recipes in this section show just how versatile chicken can be. Buy a dozen roasters at a time and use them in the following way:

Freeze two whole.

For Chicken Kiev use:

★ The breasts and wings of three chickens.

For Chicken pieces use:

★ The remainder of the three chickens, plus an additional one, cut into joints, making 12 pieces in all. Egg and breadcrumb four, wrap in double foil or polythene tissue paper, or place in foil dishes and seal with double thicknesses of foil.

Freeze eight plain or use for Country house chicken.

For Chicken curry use:

★ Two chickens jointed into 12 portions.

For Chickenburgers use:

★ The meat from one boned chicken.

For Chicken turnovers, Kromeskies, Vol-au-vent, and Pancakes use:

★ Three chickens, roasted.

For Chicken stock use:

★ All the carcasses.

Thaw the bird sufficiently to remove the giblets from the body cavity. Place on a chopping board and with a sharp knife cut through and along the length of the breastbone.

Open the bird out, then cut through along the length of the backbone. If liked, the backbone can be removed entirely by cutting along close to either side. Tap the back of the knife sharply with a heavy weight to cut the bird in half through the bony sections.

26

Lay the chicken halves skin side up on a board and halve again by cutting diagonally across between wing and thigh. The bird is now in quarters.

To make six joints divide each thigh and drumstick portion in half by cutting through at the ball and socket joint.

## Chicken curry

12 chicken pieces
seasoned flour, for coating
2 oz./50 g. lard or dripping
2 onions, peeled and chopped
1 pint/6 dl. curry sauce (see page 9)

Coat the chicken pieces in the seasoned flour. Melt the fat in a large, heavy frying pan; add the onion and cook until transparent. Transfer to a baking dish. Add the chicken pieces, a few at a time, to the fat in the pan and cook until brown on all sides.

Place the chicken in the dish with the onion, add the sauce, cover with foil. Bake in a moderate oven (350°F., 180°C., Gas Mark 4) for 1 hour.

**To freeze:** Cool rapidly and pack into suitable containers.

**To prepare for serving:** Reheat, unthawed, in a saucepan. Serve with plain boiled rice. *Makes 12 portions.*

## Chickenburgers

3 slices white bread
1 lb./450 g. shoulder of veal, skinned
1 3-lb./1¼-kg. chicken, boned
¼ pint/1½ dl. milk
½ teaspoon salt
¼ teaspoon nutmeg
1 large egg

Soak the bread in the milk. Trim the veal and cut the chicken into pieces. Mince the meats finely. Mix in the bread and all the remaining ingredients. Divide into 12 portions and shape into patties.

**To freeze:** Wrap in double or heavy duty foil. Use dividers between the layers if to be stacked. Seal and freeze.

**To prepare for serving:** Shallow-fry thawed or frozen, in plenty of butter or oil. *Makes 12.*

## Chicken turnovers

12 oz./350 g. puff pastry
12 oz./350 g. cooked chicken, finely chopped
1 small onion, finely chopped
1 10½-oz./298-g. can condensed mushroom soup
1 tablespoon chopped parsley, blanched
½ teaspoon salt
dash Worcestershire sauce

Roll the pastry to ⅛-inch (3-mm.) thickness. Cut into 5-inch (13-cm.) circles, using a saucer. Combine the remaining ingredients and put a spoonful of filling into the centre of each pastry circle. Damp the edges and seal with the prongs of a fork.

**To freeze:** Pack into foil or plastic containers. Cover closely and seal before freezing.

**To prepare for serving:** Put the turnovers, unthawed, on a wet baking sheet, brush with beaten egg and cook in a very hot oven (450°F., 230°C., Gas Mark 8) for 30 minutes. *Makes 12.*

Scrape back the meat from the wing bone.

Place a portion of butter in the centre of each breast.

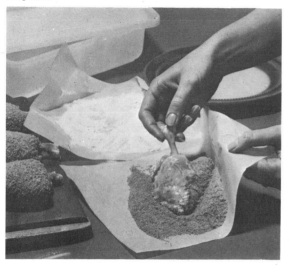

Dip in beaten egg and coat with crumbs.

Chicken Kiev

## Chicken Kiev

3 whole chicken breasts, with wings attached
6 oz./175 g. parsley butter
salt and pepper to taste
seasoned flour
1 egg, lightly beaten
toasted breadcrumbs for coating

To remove the chicken breasts, skin the chicken and place with the front facing you. Using a sharp filleting knife, carefully remove the flesh from one side of the breast bone, without piercing the meat. Gradually work the tip of the knife down towards the wing. Sever the tendon between the ball and socket wing-joint and cut through the skin underneath it. Repeat this process on the other side of the chicken. Treat the two other chickens in the same way. Cut off the two end bones from each

wing, scrape back the meat from the remaining bone (see pictures).

Put each chicken breast between two sheets of wet greaseproof paper and pound until thin, taking care not to split the meat. Roll the butter, cut into six equal portions and place one in the centre of each breast.

Sprinkle with salt and pepper. Roll up envelope fashion, letting the wing bone protrude. Toss each roll in well-seasoned flour; dip into the egg and coat with crumbs.

**To freeze:** Pack in a plastic container, cover closely and freeze.

**To prepare for serving:** Thaw overnight in the refrigerator. Deep-fry in hot oil, drain and serve. Garnish with parsley and top with a little extra parsley butter if liked. *Serves 6.*

## Kromeskies

1 lb./450 g. cooked chicken
8 oz./225 g. cooked ham or bacon
3 oz./75 g. margarine
1 large onion, peeled and finely chopped
1 clove garlic, crushed
3 oz./75 g. flour
¾ pint/4 dl. chicken stock or 1 stock cube and water
2 tablespoons tomato ketchup
salt and pepper to taste
¼ teaspoon powdered mace
12 rashers streaky bacon, trimmed

Put the chicken and ham through a fine mincer. Melt the margarine in a saucepan and add the onion and garlic. Cook gently until soft but not brown. Stir in the flour and cook for 1 minute, gradually add the stock. Add all the other ingredients, with the exception of the bacon. Bring to the boil and cook gently, beating with a wooden spoon, until the mixture begins to leave the sides of the pan. Spread into a sandwich tin and leave to cool. Meanwhile, stretch the bacon by smoothing it with a dinner knife and cut each rasher in half. When the mixture is quite cold, divide it into 24 equal portions. Flour both hands and roll each portion into a ball and then into a cork shape. Wrap a piece of bacon around each.

**To freeze:** Arrange in oblong plastic or foil containers. Stack layers on top of each other, with foil or polythene tissue paper dividers between. Seal and freeze.

**To prepare for serving:** Thaw at room temperature, allowing approximately 2 hours. Toss in seasoned flour, dip in coating batter and deep-fry in hot fat (380°F., 193°C.) for 2–3 minutes. *Makes 3 servings for 4.*

## Chicken stock

*To each 1 lb./450 g. chicken bones and trimmings use:*
3 pints/1¾ litres water
1 small carrot, sliced
1 small onion, stuck with a clove
small bouquet garni

Wash the carcasses and trimmings. Place in a large saucepan and add the water. Bring slowly to the boil and simmer for 2 hours. Skim frequently to remove the fat from the surface of the stock and the sides of the pan. Add the remaining ingredients and enough cold water to replace that which has evaporated. Simmer gently for another hour. Skim again and strain the stock through a muslin cloth.

Put the stock into a clean pan; add the vegetables and bouquet garni. Return to the boil and simmer for another 30 minutes. Remove any remaining scum with kitchen paper.

**To freeze:** Cool and strain into plastic containers or polythene bags leaving a 1-inch (2½-cm.) headspace. Separate cubes, frozen in an ice cube tray from the refrigerator, supply just enough strong stock to improve a gravy or sauce.

**To prepare for serving:** Heat in a saucepan and use as a base for soups or sauces.

## Vol-au-vent filling

1½ pints/scant litre milk
1 small onion
blade mace
4 oz./100 g. butter or margarine
3 oz./75 g. flour
1 green pepper, de-seeded
8 oz./225 g. button mushrooms, quartered
1¼ lb./575 g. cooked chicken, diced
salt and pepper to taste

Warm the milk with the onion and mace. Allow to infuse for 30 minutes, then strain. Melt 3 oz. (75 g.) of the butter in a saucepan; stir in the flour and cook gently for a further 2 minutes. Draw the pan off the heat and whisk in the milk. Blanch the green pepper in boiling water for 7 minutes. Immerse in cold water to cool. Cut into ¼-inch (½-cm.) dice.

Heat the remaining butter in a small saucepan; add the pepper and mushrooms and cook for 1½ minutes. Add, together with the chicken, to the sauce. Return the pan to the heat, bring to the boil and cook for a further 2 minutes, stirring continuously. Season to taste.

**To freeze:** Cool rapidly and pack into a large plastic bowl if required for a forthcoming party, or into several small containers if the filling is required for family meals.

**To prepare for serving:** Thaw either in the refrigerator or at room temperature. The time required depends on the size of the container. Reheat in a saucepan before filling the vol-au-vent cases. *Fills 12 large cases.*

## Country house chicken

8 chicken pieces
2 tablespoons seasoned flour
2 oz./50 g. butter
8 oz./225 g. button mushrooms
2 chicken stock cubes
¾ pint/4 dl. boiling water
4 tablespoons dry sherry
2 teaspoons cornflour
1 tablespoon orange jelly marmalade

Turn the chicken pieces in the seasoned flour. Heat half the butter in a flameproof casserole and sauté the chicken pieces gently until golden brown all over. Cover and continue cooking gently, turning frequently, for 20 minutes. In a separate pan, sauté the mushrooms in the remaining butter for 3 minutes, slicing the larger ones. Dissolve the stock cubes in the boiling water, stir in sherry, cornflour moistened with a little cold water and the marmalade. Add the mushrooms to the chicken, strain the liquid over them. Bring to the boil, cover and simmer for a further 5 minutes. Cool.

**To freeze:** Pack in plastic containers. Seal and label.

**To prepare for serving:** De-frost, turn into a saucepan, reheat gently to boiling point and simmer for 10 minutes. Stir frequently to prevent burning. *Serves 4–6.*

**Note:** This dish is also excellent made with frozen chicken for re-freezing or for serving immediately.

## Basic pancakes

8 oz./225 g. plain flour
½ teaspoon salt
4 eggs
1 pint/6 dl. milk
4 teaspoons corn oil
oil for frying

Sieve the flour and salt into a basin. Lightly beat the eggs, add to the dry ingredients and gradually beat in the milk, until the batter is smooth. Finally beat in the corn oil. Heat a little oil in a small pan and use to fry small thin pancakes until golden brown on both sides.

**To freeze:** Cool and pack together in layers with polythene tissue, double or heavy duty foil dividers. Place in a polythene bag. Seal and label.

**To prepare for serving:** Uncover and thaw at room temperature for 30 minutes, spread out. To reheat, place on baking trays and put into a moderately hot oven (400°F., 200°C., Gas Mark 6) for 10 minutes. *Makes about 36.*

## Chicken pancakes

*For the filling:*
2 oz./50 g. butter
1 large onion, peeled and finely chopped
2 oz./50 g. flour
1 pint/6 dl. chicken stock or milk
1 lb./450 g. cooked chicken, finely minced
salt and pepper to taste
dash Worcestershire sauce
36 small thin pancakes
1 pint/6 dl. tomato sauce (see page 9)
12 oz./350 g. cheese, grated

Melt the butter in a saucepan, add the onion and cook until soft. Gradually stir in the flour and cook gently for 2 minutes, add the stock or milk, bring to the boil and cook for a further 2 minutes, stirring constantly. Stir in the remaining ingredients. Allow the mixture to cool, then spoon a little of the filling into each thawed pancake. Roll and pack closely in foil-lined dishes. Cover with tomato sauce (see page 9) and sprinkle with grated cheese.

**To freeze:** Cover with foil and partially freeze. When the pancakes are sufficiently solid, lift out of the dishes and wrap in double or heavy duty foil. Seal and return to the freezer.

**To prepare for serving:** Unwrap the pancakes and return to their original dishes. Thaw at room temperature allowing approximately 5 hours. Cook in a moderately hot oven (375°F., 190°C., Gas Mark 5) for 30–40 minutes. *Makes 3–4 servings for 4.*

## APPLE CHAIN

Buy 16 lb. (7 kg.) cooking apples. If they are slightly damaged, buy a few extra pounds and discard the bruised parts. Use half for the Basic apple purée recipe, then pack in ¼- or ½-pint (1½- or 3-dl.) containers. These small packs can be thawed quickly without waste for use in puddings, sauces or as baby food.

Use the remainder of the apples sliced. A few can be stored with blackberries – by the dry pack method – for pies or to serve as stewed fruit. Store some slices in plain syrup packs and some unsweetened, but for convenience store the largest portion in dry sugar packs. Use these for puddings and pies.

## Basic apple purée

8 lb./3½ kg. cooking apples
½ pint/3 dl. water
2 oz./50 g. butter or margarine
juice and zest of 1 lemon
8 oz./225 g. granulated sugar

Wash and quarter the apples. Put them into a large saucepan or preserving pan without peeling or coring. Add the water, butter or margarine, lemon juice and zest. Cover with a lid or piece of aluminium foil. Cook gently, shaking the pan from time to time. When the apples are almost pulped add the sugar and then beat with a wooden spoon until completely smooth. Continue to cook until the sugar is completely dissolved. Rub the mixture through a fine hair or nylon sieve and discard the peel and cores.

**To freeze:** Pour the purée into cream cartons, plastic or other suitable containers, leaving a ½-inch (1-cm.) headspace. For convenience, pack in small quantities, just enough for one serving or to suit your family's needs. Seal and freeze.

**To prepare for serving:** Either thaw at room temperature (the length of time required depends on the size and shape of the container) or place the container under hot running water to loosen. Turn the contents into a saucepan and heat.

Packing basic apple purée

## Apple snow

sugar to taste
½ pint/3 dl. basic apple purée, thawed
green colouring
2 egg whites

Add the sugar to the apple purée and tint with a little green colouring but be careful not to add too much. Whisk the egg whites stiffly and fold into the apples. Spoon into individual dishes and chill; and, if liked, garnish with apple slices before serving. *Serves 4.*

Apple snow

## Apple fool

¼ pint/1½ dl. custard, cold
½ pint/3 dl. basic apple purée, thawed
sugar to taste

Mix the custard into the apple purée. Sweeten to taste and spoon into individual dishes. Chill before serving. *Serves 4.*

## Baked apple soufflé

3 oz./75 g. castor sugar
pinch ground cinnamon
½ pint/3 dl. basic apple purée, thawed
2 large eggs, separated

Mix the sugar and cinnamon into the apple purée then beat in the egg yolks. Whisk the egg whites stiffly and fold into the mixture using a metal spoon. Spoon into a heavily greased 1½-pint (1-litre) soufflé or pie dish. Bake in the centre of a moderate oven (350°F., 180°C., Gas Mark 4) for 30–40 minutes or until firm to the touch and golden brown. Serve at once with cream or custard. *Serves 4.*

## Apple cheese flan

6 oz./175 g. shortcrust pastry
2 eggs, lightly whisked
3 oz./75 g. castor sugar
finely grated rind of ½ lemon
¼ pint/1½ dl. basic apple purée, thawed

Line an 8-inch (20-cm.) flan or loose-based sandwich tin with the pastry. Prick the base and bake blind, in a pre-heated hot oven (400°F., 200°C., Gas Mark 6) for 15 minutes. Meanwhile, beat the eggs, sugar and lemon rind into the apple purée.

Remove the flan from the oven and lower the heat to 350°F., 180°C., Gas Mark 4. Pour the filling into the case. Continue to cook for 30–35 minutes or until the filling is firm. Serve hot or cold. *Serves 6.*

## Apple slices

Peel and core 8 lb. (3½ kg.) apples and cut into ½-inch (1-cm.) slices. Blanch in boiling water for 1 minute, and pack into polythene bags or other suitable containers. Seal and freeze.

**To prepare for serving:** Partially thaw in the sealed container, at room temperature.

Packing apple slices

## Apple and sultana layer pudding

3 oz./75 g. self-raising flour
pinch salt
¼ teaspoon mixed spice
1½ oz./40 g. white breadcrumbs
2 oz./50 g. shredded suet
3–4 tablespoons milk
*For the filling:*
8 oz./225 g. apple slices, partially thawed
2 oz./50 g. sultanas
2 oz./50 g. brown sugar
rind of ½ lemon, finely grated

Sieve the flour, salt and mixed spice into a mixing bowl. Stir in the breadcrumbs and suet. Add sufficient milk to make a soft, scone-like dough. Divide into three unequal portions. Prepare the filling by finely chopping the apple slices. Mix with the remaining ingredients. Grease a 1-pint (6-dl.) pudding basin and pat out the smallest piece of suet pastry to fit the base of the bowl. Add half the fruit filling and pat out the second piece of pastry to cover this. Add the rest of the filling and pat out the remaining pastry to cover it. Cover the basin with a piece of foil. Steam for 1½–1¾ hours. Serve with custard. *Serves 4.*

Apple charlotte

## Apple pie

8 oz./225 g. shortcrust pastry

12 oz./350 g. apple slices, partially thawed

2 oz./50 g. castor sugar

3 whole cloves

*To decorate:*

beaten egg white or milk

castor sugar

Divide the pastry into two pieces, one slightly smaller than the other. Knead each to a smooth ball. Roll the smaller piece very thinly, to fit an 8–8½-inch (20–21-cm.) pie plate. Cover the plate with the pastry and press out all the air bubbles, starting from the centre.

Put a thick layer of apple over the pastry; sprinkle with castor sugar and add the cloves. Pile the remaining apple slices on top and smooth to a flat dome. Damp the edges of the pastry. Roll the remaining pastry and, without stretching it, cover the top of the pie. Press the edges together to seal; trim and flute. Make a small vent in the centre, brush with milk or lightly beaten egg white and sprinkle with castor sugar. Bake in the centre of a moderate oven (350°F., 180°C., Gas Mark 4) for 30–40 minutes.  *Serves 4.*

## Apple charlotte

12 oz./350 g. apple slices, partially thawed

3 oz./75 g. breadcrumbs

1 oz./25 g. brown sugar

1 tablespoon golden syrup

grated rind and juice of ½ lemon

Grease a ¾-pint (4-dl.) pie dish and arrange the apple slices and breadcrumbs in alternate layers, starting and finishing with breadcrumbs. Warm the remaining ingredients in a small saucepan, to blend. Spoon the syrup over the crumbs. Bake in the centre of a warm oven (325°F., 170°C., Gas Mark 3) for 50–60 minutes. Garnish with grated lemon rind.  *Serves 4.*

33

## Apple blintzes

8 fl. oz./2¼ dl. milk

4 eggs

1 teaspoon salt

4 oz./100 g. plain flour

oil, for greasing pan

*For the filling:*

1½ lb./675 g. cottage cheese, drained

pinch salt

½ oz./15 g. butter

2 tablespoons castor sugar

8 oz./225 g. apple slices, partially thawed

To make the batter, beat together lightly the milk, salt and eggs. Beat in the flour until smooth. Heat a griddle or heavy shallow pan and grease lightly with oil. Spread about 2 tablespoons of the batter evenly over the griddle and cook until bubbles form on the surface. Turn and cook the other side.

To make the filling, press the cheese through a sieve, or mash with a fork. Add salt to taste, add the butter and castor sugar and beat well together. Place one or two apple slices and a tablespoon of filling in the centre of each pancake and fold envelope style.

**To freeze:** Pack in a plastic container in layers with polythene tissue, double or heavy duty foil dividers. Seal and freeze.

**To prepare for serving:** Thaw. Fry in melted butter until golden brown on both sides. Serve with soured cream into which an equal quantity of warmed apricot jam has been stirred. *Serves 4–6.*

## Eve's pudding

12 oz./350 g. apple slices, partially thawed

3 oz./75 g. castor sugar

4 oz./100 g. plain flour

1½ teaspoons baking powder

pinch salt

2 oz./50 g. margarine

1 egg

¼ teaspoon vanilla essence

2–3 tablespoons milk

Mix the apple slices with 1 oz. (25 g.) of the castor sugar and arrange them in a 1-pint (6-dl.) pie dish. Sieve the flour, baking powder and salt. Add the remaining sugar and fat, cut into pieces, to the flour. Rub in until the mixture resembles fine breadcrumbs. Beat the egg lightly with the vanilla essence. Mix into the fat and flour with sufficient milk to make a creamy consistency.

Spread the mixture over the surface of the apples and bake in a moderate oven (350°F., 180°C., Gas Mark 4) for 40 minutes. *Serves 4.*

# Chapter Three

# Buffet parties

This kind of party has long been popular as the relaxed, easy way to entertain. The guests do most of the work once the party has started, helping themselves to plates, cutlery and food. However, it does presuppose that the hostess has lots of time on her hands for preparing the food beforehand.

You, the fortunate freezer owner, can spend an hour or two on several different days making up the provisions for the buffet table! You can also serve a frozen sweet straight from the freezer to add a dramatic touch to the festivities when the more solid titbits have disappeared and appetites are flagging. How else could you produce 15 or 20 frozen Orange cups, each nestling in the skin of the orange and gleaming with frost, whenever you want to? Most of the recipes in the following section serve 15, as this is a fair average number for such a party.

If you are serving 15 guests, a selection of seven recipes should be adequate in quantity – two sweet, four cold savoury and one hot savoury should be an ideal balance of dishes. For fewer numbers, drop one savoury recipe, and for more, increase the selection, bearing in mind that most guests will average seven selections from the buffet table. (Greedy guests will eat more, but then there may be a few who will be too busy talking to eat as many.)

Another advantage which the freezer bestows is that you can prepare more than you think you will need and only completely thaw sufficient to set a generous table at the start of the party. If the food vanishes more rapidly than you had expected, you produce your extra supplies from the refrigerator. But if they are not needed, they can remain happily in the freezer for another day.

## Onion bread rolls

$\frac{1}{2}$ pint/3 dl. tepid water
$\frac{1}{2}$ oz./15 g. dried yeast
1 teaspoon sugar
2 tablespoons corn oil
1 lb./450 g. plain flour
1 packet French onion soup

Pour the water on to the yeast. Add the sugar and leave until the yeast has dissolved. Stir in the corn oil and mix well. Sieve the flour into a mixing bowl and add the contents of the packet of soup. Stir in the liquid and mix to form a soft dough, adding a little more water if necessary. Beat the dough until it leaves the sides of the bowl clean. Cover with a damp cloth and leave to rise in a warm place, until double in bulk. Turn out and knead lightly.

Divide the dough into 15 equal portions and shape into rolls. Place on a greased baking sheet and leave to prove in a warm place for 10–15 minutes. Bake in a hot oven (425°F., 220°C., Gas Mark 7) for 10–15 minutes.

**To freeze:** Cool and pack in polythene bags. Seal tightly and freeze.

**To prepare for serving:** Thaw at room temperature in the sealed bag. *Makes 15.*

## Hamburger patties

2 lb./900 g. lean chuck steak
1 onion, peeled
1 clove garlic
2 slices bread
1 egg
1 teaspoon salt
pinch pepper
$\frac{1}{4}$ teaspoon sage

Remove all fat from the steak, mince it twice with

the onion and garlic, using a coarse cutter. At the end of the second mincing, add the bread, so that this goes through the mincer last. Turn the meat into a basin, add the beaten egg and seasoning. Mix well. Form into cakes about 3 inches ($7\frac{1}{2}$ cm.) across and $\frac{1}{4}$ inch ($\frac{1}{2}$ cm.) thick.

**To freeze:** Arrange four patties in a row, put a dividing piece of foil on top; continue to stack with foil dividers between each layer. Wrap tightly in double foil, seal and freeze.

**To prepare for serving:** Partially thaw in the refrigerator, allowing 5 hours. Pat dry mustard into the surface before grilling. Baste well with barbecue sauce while cooking. Sandwich hot patties between halves of soft rolls with more mustard and any good pickles, or relishes, or thin slices of onion. *Makes 16–18 patties.*

## Savoury sandwich loaf

1 large white loaf, unsliced
2 eggs, hard-boiled
$\frac{1}{4}$ pint/1$\frac{1}{2}$ dl. single cream
2 oz./50 g. butter
salt and pepper
squeeze lemon juice
green colouring
1 tablespoon spinach purée
1 2-oz./57-g. jar lobster paste
3 packets demi-sel cheese

Remove the outside crust from the bread and then slice lengthways horizontally into four. Using a fork, mash the hard-boiled eggs, while still warm, with 1 tablespoon of the cream and $\frac{1}{2}$ oz. (15 g.) of the butter. Season well. Beat the remaining butter with a squeeze of lemon juice to soften and add a little green colouring. Add the spinach purée. Spread the first piece of bread with the lobster paste, and cover with a second piece. Spread with the egg mixture and cover with the third layer. Spread this one with the spinach butter and cover with the top layer of bread. Blend together the demi-sel cheese and the remaining cream until soft and of a spreading consistency. Completely cover the loaf with the cream cheese mixture and smooth with a palette knife. Chill and slice, using a sharp knife. Reshape into a loaf.

**To freeze:** Pack in a suitable plastic container. Seal and freeze.

**To prepare for serving:** Thaw, covered, at room temperature, allowing approximately 5 hours. Cut each slice in half lengthways. *Makes 15 slices.*

## Sausage rolls

2 7-oz./198-g. packets puff pastry
12 oz./350 g. pork or beef sausage meat
salt and pepper

Roll one packet of pastry thinly to approximately 12 by 6 inches (30 by 15 cm.). Trim the edges with a knife and cut in half lengthways. Season the sausage meat well, divide in half and roll one portion into two long rolls the same length as the pastry. Place down the centre of each strip. Brush one side of the pastry with a little water, fold over and seal. Using a sharp knife, cut each strip into six sausage rolls. Make up the other packet of pastry and the remaining sausage meat in the same way.

**To freeze:** Chill until the pastry is firm. Stack in layers, with foil or polythene tissue dividing papers. Seal and freeze.

**To prepare for serving:** Place the frozen sausage rolls on wet baking sheets. Cook in a very hot oven (450°F., 230°C., Gas Mark 8) for 10 minutes. Reduce the temperature to 425°F., 220°C., Gas Mark 7 for a further 10 minutes. *Makes 24.*

## Cheese and apple horns

1$\frac{1}{2}$ lb./675 g. shortcrust pastry, flavoured with
  1 oz./25 g. Parmesan cheese, grated
1 egg, beaten
1 oz./25 g. extra Parmesan cheese, grated

Roll the pastry to an oblong and trim to 14 by 4$\frac{1}{2}$ inches (35 by 10 cm.), then cut into six strips each $\frac{3}{4}$ inch (2 cm.) wide. Wind overlapping around the horn tins. Place on a baking sheet, with the pastry ends underneath. Brush with egg, sprinkle with the extra Parmesan cheese. Bake in a fairly hot oven (400°F., 200°C., Gas Mark 6) for 15–20 minutes. Cool on a wire tray.

**To freeze:** Pack in a large plastic container. Seal and freeze.

**To prepare for serving:** Thaw, covered, at room temperature allowing approximately 5 hours. Fill with grated apple and cream cheese. *Makes 18–20.*

Cheese and apple horns

Tuna pâté

## Tuna pâté

2 7-oz./198-g. cans tuna steak
little milk
blade mace
small piece bay leaf
sprig parsley
4 black peppercorns
1 oz./25 g. butter
2 oz./50 g. flour
4 tablespoons single cream or top of milk
1–2 teaspoons lemon juice
few gherkins, finely chopped (optional)

Drain the liquor from the tuna and make up to ½ pint (3 dl.) with milk. Place in a saucepan with the mace, bay leaf, parsley sprig and peppercorns. Leave over a gentle heat to infuse for 15 minutes, then bring to the boil and strain. Melt the butter in a small saucepan and stir in the flour. Cook for 2–3 minutes, add the milk mixture and bring to the boil, stirring; cook for 2 minutes. Mash the tuna fish with a fork, add to the sauce with the cream, lemon juice and gherkins and mix well together. Add additional seasoning if necessary. Place in a foil-lined serving dish and leave in a cool place to set.

**To freeze:** Cover with foil and partially freeze. When sufficiently solid, remove from the container and over-wrap with double foil.

**To prepare for serving:** Unwrap and return to the original serving dish. Thaw at room temperature allowing approximately 2 hours. Decorate with parsley and lemon. *Serves 16.*

## Kidney risotto

3 tablespoons cooking oil
2 large onions, peeled and thinly sliced
2 cloves garlic, crushed with 2 teaspoons salt
2 lb./900 g. Patna rice
3 pints/1¾ litres chicken stock or 3 stock cubes and water
3 green peppers, de-seeded and sliced
2 oz./50 g. butter
8 lambs' kidneys, trimmed and sliced
12 oz./350 g. mushrooms, quartered

Heat the oil in a large saucepan, add the onions and garlic and cook over a low heat until soft but not brown. Add the rice and fry for 2 minutes before adding the stock. Bring to the boil, cover with a lid and simmer, very gently, for 10 minutes. Add the peppers and cook for a further 10 minutes. Heat the butter in a frying pan and gently sauté the kidneys; remove from the pan and replace with the mushrooms, cook for 2 minutes.

**To freeze:** Cool all the ingredients, then toss the kidneys and mushrooms in the rice. Spoon into large plastic containers or polythene bags, seal and freeze.

**To prepare for serving:** Immerse containers in hot water to loosen the contents. Turn into meat dishes, cover with foil and reheat in a warm oven (325°F., 170°C., Gas Mark 3). Place in serving dishes, sprinkle with grated cheese. *Serves 15.*

Arrange alternate layers of lasagne, cheese and sauce and sprinkle the top with grated cheese.

The trays can either be frozen separately or with one turned upside down on top of another. If you up-turn them, only one need be covered with foil. Partially freeze, then place together.

Seal the joining edges of the two trays with freezer tape. Don't use ordinary adhesive tape as it doesn't stand up to low temperatures.

As you go round the edge with the tape, pinch the trays together to make sure the tape sticks properly to ensure a good seal.

# Lasagne

1 2 lb. 3-oz./992-g. can tomatoes

1 pint tomato sauce (see page 9)

1 teaspoon salt

$\frac{1}{4}$ teaspoon pepper

4 tablespoons oil

2 large onions, sliced

1 clove garlic, crushed

2 lb./900 g. minced beef

2 1-lb./454-g. packets lasagne

3 8-oz./226-g. cartons cottage cheese

4 oz./100 g. Parmesan cheese, grated

Combine the tomatoes, tomato sauce, salt and pepper in a saucepan. Bring to simmering point and cover with a lid. Heat 3 tablespoons of the oil in a frying pan, add the onion and garlic and cook until soft but not brown. Stir the meat into the onion and cook briskly to brown. Spoon the meat into the tomato sauce and simmer, uncovered, for 1 hour. Add the remaining oil to a large saucepan (or preserving pan) of salted, boiling water. Add the lasagne and cook, at boiling point, for 12 minutes. Drain and separate the pieces.

**To freeze:** Use foil dishes or line serving dishes with foil, spoon a little meat sauce into the base of each. Divide the cottage cheese, allowing equal proportions for each dish. Arrange alternate layers of lasagne, cottage cheese and sauce, finishing with the sauce. Sprinkle the top of each with grated cheese. Cover with foil and partially freeze. Remove from the containers and re-wrap in double or heavy duty foil. Return to the freezer.

**To prepare for serving:** Remove the foil and transfer to the original serving dishes. Thaw at room temperature. Cook in a moderate oven (350°F., 180°C., Gas Mark 4) for 30–40 minutes. *Serves 15.*

# Party tartlets

Bake blind your usual rich shortcrust pastry tartlet cases. When cold, stack them together, place them in suitable containers, seal, label and freeze. When you are ready to use them, remove from the freezer and allow them to come to room temperature before crisping a little in the oven. Now add a hot savoury or sweet filling.

Raw pastry tartlet cases can be kept equally well in the freezer and are simply baked when required. However, for a party you will save a little time by baking them before freezing.

Small fruit tartlets are also excellent for buffet parties. Instead of a rich shortcrust pastry, use a biscuit crust mixture to make them more unusual. Here is a good basic savoury filling.

## Basic savoury filling

1 oz./25 g. butter
1 tablespoon flour
¼ pint/1½ dl. chicken stock
2–3 oz./50–75 g. button mushrooms, washed but unpeeled
small nut butter
1 tablespoon water
1 teaspoon lemon juice
6 oz./175 g. cooked chicken or turkey, cut finely
2 tablespoons cooked peas
1 4½-oz./128-g. can pimento, cut in thin strips
    1 inch/2½ cm. long and drained

Melt the butter and stir in the flour to make a smooth roux. Remove from the heat, stir in chicken stock and cook for a few minutes. Meanwhile, slice the mushrooms and cook them, covered, in a little butter, water and lemon juice. Add the mushrooms to the sauce together with the chicken or turkey. Add the peas and pimento. Heat through. Fill the tartlet cases straight away and serve while still hot.

This filling can be made in advance and freezes well. When you are ready to use it, allow to thaw and then heat through before filling the warmed tartlet cases.

The basic savoury mixture can be varied in several ways. For instance, instead of chicken or turkey, use shelled shrimps or a can of crab meat, flaked, or tuna, or salmon. Or, if you have any cooked salmon in the freezer, flake it roughly and use as the basis of the recipe.

## Orange cups

3 lemons
10 oranges, halved
water
1 lb./450 g. granulated sugar
4 egg whites

Pare the skin off one lemon and five orange halves. Squeeze out and reserve the juice of all the oranges and lemons, taking care not to split the orange cases. Set 15 orange halves aside. Add water to the fruit juice to make 2½ pints (1½ litres) and place in a large saucepan with the pared skin. Dissolve the sugar in the liquid over gentle heat. Bring to the boil and continue to boil rapidly, without stirring, for 12 minutes. Cool and strain into a large mixing bowl. Freeze for 6 hours. To prepare the orange cases, insert the handle of a teaspoon between the pith and skin of each orange. Loosen the pith all the way round each case. Discard the pith. Break the prepared sorbet into pieces with a fork, and then mash. Whisk the egg whites stiffly and fold into the sorbet. Spoon into the prepared cases and return to the freezer with the remaining sorbet. Top each orange case with a scoop of the remaining sorbet before serving. *Serves 15.*

## Pear Hélène tartlets

3 oz./75 g. castor sugar
½ pint/3 dl. water
4 pears, peeled, cored and cut into quarters
juice of ½ lemon
8 oz./225 g. plain chocolate, melted
1 tablespoon oil
ice cream, for filling
15 frozen tartlet cases, thawed

Dissolve the sugar in the water, bring to the boil and continue to boil rapidly for 5 minutes. Lower the heat and simmer the pears in the syrup until tender, do not allow them to break. Drain, cool and sprinkle with lemon juice.

Add the oil to the melted chocolate and keep it warm.

Just before serving, put a scoop of ice cream in each case, top with a piece of pear and drizzle melted chocolate over. *Makes 15.*

## Gingered pear coupes

1 quantity buttered crumbs (see below)
3 16-oz./454-g. containers frozen sliced pears in sugar
   syrup
6 tablespoons ginger syrup
¾ pint/4 dl. double cream
sugar to taste
3 egg whites
12 small pieces stem ginger

De-frost the containers of buttered crumbs and pears in warm water. Divide half the crumbs between 12 coupe glasses. Arrange the pear slices upright over the crumb base, and pour over the ginger syrup and a little syrup from the frozen pears. Fill up the coupes to the level of the top of the pear slices with more buttered crumbs. Whip the cream and sweeten to taste. Fold in the stiffly beaten egg white and spoon or pipe cream over the crumbs and fruit. Decorate with the stem ginger. *Serves 12.*

## Sweet buttered crumbs

These can be used in a number of recipes with fruit and fruit purées. Make up a basic quantity as follows and freeze in four small plastic containers.

4 oz./100 g. unsalted butter
12 oz./350 g. dried white crumbs
4 oz./100 g. demerara sugar

Melt the butter, stir in the breadcrumbs and fry until beginning to turn brown. Add the sugar and continue frying until the mixture is golden brown, stirring constantly. Cool.

**To freeze:** Pack in plastic containers.

**To prepare for use:** Thaw in warm water.

## Pear condé

2 15-oz./425-g. cans creamed rice pudding
2 30-oz./850-g. containers pear halves in sugar syrup
4 tablespoons apricot jam
½ pint/3 dl. double cream
16 chocolate leaves (see note)

Place the creamed rice in the base of two shallow serving dishes. De-frost the containers of pears in warm water. Drain the pears well and arrange, cut side down, over the rice. Heat the pear syrup with the jam, allow to cool slightly and strain over the pears to glaze. Whip the cream, pipe a border of rosettes all around the dish and between the pear halves. Decorate with chocolate leaves. *Serves 15.*

**Note:** To make chocolate leaves, melt plain chocolate in a small bowl over hot water. Choose even-size rose leaves and wash and dry carefully. Using the back of a teaspoon coat the underside of the leaves with melted chocolate. Allow to cool until quite hard then gently ease off the leaves.

## Chocolate and lime crunch pie

1 oz./25 g. butter
4 tablespoons golden syrup
8 oz./225 g. cornflakes
6 oz./175 g. plain chocolate, melted
*For the filling:*
2 packets lime jelly
¾ pint/4 dl. evaporated milk
few drops green food colouring
*To decorate:*
whipped cream
angelica leaves

Melt the butter and golden syrup together. Add to the cornflakes with the melted chocolate. Toss together lightly until well coated. Line two 8-inch (20-cm.) pie plates and allow to set. Meanwhile dissolve the jellies in ½ pint (3 dl.) boiling water and allow to cool. When nearly at setting point, whisk the evaporated milk until thick and frothy. Fold in the jelly and a little green colouring. Pour into the flan cases and allow to set. Decorate with rosettes of whipped cream and a few angelica leaves.

**To freeze:** Open freeze until firm, wrap in foil and label.

**To prepare for serving:** Allow to de-frost, unwrapped, at room temperature. *Serves 12–15.*

# Pineapple and mallow krispie pie

2 oz./50 g. butter
4 tablespoons golden syrup
4 oz./100 g. rice krispies
*For the filling:*
12 oz./350 g. marshmallows
8 tablespoons pineapple juice
few drops yellow food colouring
2 small cans pineapple cubes, drained
½ pint/3 dl. double cream
*To decorate:*
whipped cream
few pineapple pieces

Melt the butter and the golden syrup in a pan. Add to the rice krispies and mix well. Press the mixture into two 7-inch (18-cm.) pie plates and allow to cool and harden. Melt the marshmallows in a bowl over hot water with the pineapple juice. Cool and add a little yellow colouring. Whisk the cream until thick and fold into the mallow mixture with the pineapple cubes, reserving a few for decoration. Pour into the flan case and allow to set. Decorate with a little whipped cream and a few pineapple cubes.

**To freeze:** Open freeze until firm, wrap in foil and label.

**To prepare for serving:** Allow to de-frost, un-wrapped, at room temperature. *Serves 12–15.*

# Chapter Four

# Teatime entertaining

Unexpected guests have an uncanny knack of dropping in for tea on the one day when you have nothing in the biscuit tin, and no freshly baked cakes to offer them. Such problems can be solved triumphantly with some short-term items from the freezer.

By this I mean such things as scones and tea breads, which you would not expect to keep frozen long, because they are rather bulky and have a relatively short freezer life. Cooked scones, for instance, should not be stored for more than two months, and uncooked biscuit dough for more than one month.

A basic biscuit mix can be flavoured in various ways, and each flavour stored in a Swiss roll shape, from which you cut slices of just the right thickness and bake them almost while the kettle boils. It would be worthwhile to double the quantities of the basic mix when making either, and cook a batch for instant eating and a batch to store.

Certain cakes freeze well, and all the recipes given here are freezer-tested for their qualities in retaining a 'good as new' flavour and texture when thawed after a month or more of storage.

If your home baked cakes appear, after freezing, to have a poor texture or flavour, this may be due to the choice of ingredients rather than to a fault in baking. Freshly bought flour should always be used as stale flour tends to deteriorate rapidly after freezing. Another factor which helps to retain the fresh flavour of the cake is the freshness of the fat used. Fats such as butter and margarine easily pick up cross-flavours from other foods if stored in the larder or refrigerator or simply left on an open dish in the kitchen. Eggs used in cakes for freezing ought always to be perfectly fresh and very well beaten. Again, they must be extra fresh to avoid that disappointing 'flatness' of flavour when the cake is thawed out. The beating must be thorough because egg whites

freeze more quickly than yolks and traces of un-blended egg white will give the cake an uneven texture after thawing.

If you have time, make up a few fancy sandwiches as well as the standard meal size kind, and these will add an elegant touch to a tea-party table, or will add grace to a buffet spread. They store well for several weeks.

Here's how to make dainty pinwheel sandwiches for tea parties. Cut a sandwich loaf, lengthways, into thin slices and remove the crusts. Spread each slice with different coloured suitable fillings and roll up tightly as for a Swiss roll, but *lengthways*. Give the first roll a sharp press into shape; this is needed to make the final neat circle of each sandwich.

**To freeze:** Wrap the rolls individually in waxed paper and slide them into a polythene bag, excluding as much air as possible. Fasten the end securely. These pinwheel sandwiches are now ready for a party, or (if frozen) for any time you may need them during the next few weeks.

**To prepare for serving:** Remove the pinwheels from the freezer an hour or two before they are to be cut. Unwrap each roll, and place it join side down on a bread board. Cut into $\frac{1}{4}$-inch ($\frac{1}{2}$-cm.) slices with a really sharp knife.

**Sandwich fillings**
Cream cheese with sweet pickles
Cream cheese with chopped chicken and grated lemon rind
Cream cheese with chopped salami sausage
Cream cheese and chopped dates
Peanut butter, cream cheese and chives
Blue cheese, chopped bacon and chilli sauce
Cheddar cheese, grated, with chopped olives
Cream cheese and chopped olives
Sliced ham, tongue or corned beef with finely minced onion

Cream cheese and liver pâté with Worcestershire
sauce
Chopped chicken, ham and almonds
Chopped cooked liver, crisp bacon and pickles
Chopped frankfurters and chilli sauce
Chopped prawns, cream cheese and lemon juice
Chopped prawns, cottage cheese and sweet pickles

## Flavoured butters for pinwheel sandwiches

As these sandwiches look much prettier if the
filling contrasts well in colour with the bread, the
best method is to blend the filling with the butter
for spreading so that you can see what the colour
of the finished sandwiches will be.

**Green butter:** Cream 4 oz. (100 g.) butter, work
in 1 heaped tablespoon of very finely chopped
parsley, the juice of $\frac{1}{2}$ lemon, salt and pepper to
taste.

**Anchovy butter:** Cream 4 oz. (100 g.) butter,
work in 4 chopped and pounded anchovy fillets, a
pinch of pepper and a few drops of pink food
colouring.

**Mustard butter:** Cream 4 oz. (100 g.) butter,
work in a level dessertspoon of French mustard.

**Shrimp butter:** Cream 2 oz. (50 g.) butter with a
small carton of potted shrimps (including their
own butter).

## Ginger Danish pastries

$\frac{1}{2}$ oz./15 g. yeast
$1\frac{3}{4}$ oz./35 g. castor sugar
8–12 tablespoons tepid milk
12 oz./350 g. plain flour
pinch salt
7 oz./200 g. butter
*Filling A:*
2 oz./50 g. ground almonds mixed with
　　5 pieces chopped stem ginger and
　　2 tablespoons ginger syrup
*Filling B:*
2 oz./50 g. ground almonds
5 pieces stem ginger, chopped

Cream the yeast with 1 teaspoon sugar. Pour
$\frac{1}{4}$ pint ($1\frac{1}{2}$ dl.) of the tepid milk into the yeast.
Sift the flour and salt into a bowl, add the remain-
ing sugar. Make a well in the centre and pour in
the yeast mixture. Work into the flour, adding the
remaining milk if necessary, to form a light but
dry dough. Knead until smooth.

Roll into an oblong $\frac{1}{2}$ inch (1 cm.) thick and
place knobs of butter, the size of walnuts, over
two-thirds of the surface. Fold and roll as for
rough puff pastry and repeat once. Wrap in
greaseproof paper and place in a refrigerator or
cool place for 15 minutes, or until firm. Repeat
the rolling and folding until all the butter is
worked in. Chill for 1 hour or overnight. When
firm, roll out into a square $\frac{1}{4}$ inch ($\frac{1}{2}$ cm.) thick.
Cut in half.

Spread one half with the ground almond filling
A. Roll up into a sausage shape and cut into six
pieces. Cut each slice twice, two-thirds of the
way down, and fan out. Cut the other half into
squares. Fill half the squares with chopped ginger
and nuts (filling B) and fold the corners to the
centre. Make the rest of the pastry and filling into
your favourite shapes. Place on greased baking
sheets, covered, in a warm place to prove for
10–15 minutes. When the pastries have increased
their size by half, glaze with beaten egg white.
Place in a hot oven (450°F., 230°C., Gas Mark 8)
for 15–20 minutes until golden brown. Cool on a
wire tray.

**To freeze:** Seal tightly in polythene bags.

**To prepare for serving:** Thaw at room temperature allowing approximately 2 hours. *Makes
about 15 pastries.*

Ginger Danish pastries

## Pork pie for high tea

*For the pastry:*
4 oz./100 g. plain flour
$\frac{1}{2}$ teaspoon salt
$1\frac{1}{2}$ oz./40 g. white fat or lard
2 tablespoons water
*For the filling:*
12 oz./350 g. pork sausage meat
pinch powdered sage
salt and pepper to taste

Combine the sausage meat, sage, salt and pepper, then mix thoroughly to make sure the seasonings are well mingled and set aside until the pastry has been made.

Sieve the flour and salt into a warm bowl. Measure the fat and water into a small saucepan and bring to a rolling boil. Pour immediately into the centre of the flour and mix to a smooth ball with a wooden spoon. Turn on to a board and knead until smooth. Reserving a little for the lid and decoration, shape the remainder into a round. Flatten the base and begin to shape the sides. Place the sausage meat in the centre and gradually work the pastry up round the sides to form an edge. Roll the reserved pieces out to form a lid. Damp the edge of the pie with a little beaten egg and milk and place the lid over the top. Pinch the edges to seal and snip round with scissors. Flute the edges of the pie. Make a hole in the centre and decorate with leaves made from any remaining pastry. Brush with beaten egg and fix a greased band of paper around the pie. Place the pie in the centre of a very hot oven (425°F., 220°C., Gas Mark 7) for 20 minutes, then lower the heat to 350°F., 150°C., Gas Mark 4 and bake for a further 40 minutes. After 30 minutes remove the band of paper and brush the whole pie with beaten egg.

**To freeze:** Allow to become completely cold. Wrap in a double thickness of foil and seal well.

**To prepare for serving:** Thaw at room temperature allowing at least 8 hours. *Serves 6.*

## Basic biscuit dough

1 lb./450 g. plain flour and
  1 teaspoon baking powder
8 oz./225 g. butter or margarine
8 oz./225 g. castor sugar
2 eggs, beaten
$\frac{1}{2}$ teaspoon vanilla essence
little milk
$\frac{1}{2}$ teaspoon coffee essence

Sieve the flour and baking powder on to a piece of paper. Cream together the butter and sugar until light and fluffy. Add the beaten eggs, a little at a time, alternately with a few spoonfuls of sifted flour. Mix in the rest of the flour. Divide the mixture in half. Add the vanilla essence to one half and work it into the dough with sufficient milk to make a firm paste. Add the coffee flavouring to the other half of the mixture and work into the dough in the same way.

**To freeze:** Form each portion into a roll, and wrap in polythene tissue paper or aluminium foil. Seal and freeze.

**To prepare for cooking:** Thaw at room temperature until the roll is soft enough to slice into $\frac{1}{4}$-inch ($\frac{1}{2}$-cm.) slices and bake in a moderately hot oven (375°F., 190°C., Gas Mark 5) for 10–15 minutes. If liked decorate by lightly pressing a glacé cherry or almond in the centre.

## One-stage peanut cookies

6 oz./175 g. plain flour
$\frac{1}{2}$ teaspoon baking powder
$\frac{3}{4}$ teaspoon bicarbonate of soda
$\frac{1}{4}$ teaspoon salt
4 oz./100 g. luxury margarine
3 tablespoons peanut butter
3 oz./75 g. castor sugar
3 oz./75 g. soft brown sugar
1 standard egg

Sieve the flour, baking powder, bicarbonate of soda and salt into a mixing bowl. Place the remaining ingredients in the bowl and beat together with a wooden spoon until well mixed (approximately 2–3 minutes). Gather the mixture together with the fingertips and form into a roll.

**To freeze:** Cut the roll into four pieces and place dividing papers between them. Wrap the rolls in paper or aluminium foil. If wrapped in polythene tissue paper, seal before freezing.

**To prepare for cooking:** Unwrap and thaw at room temperature until the dough is soft enough to slice. Cut thinly and place fairly far apart on a greased baking sheet. Bake in the centre of a moderately hot oven (375° F., 190°C., Gas Mark 5) for 7–10 minutes. Cool on a wire tray and then dip the cookies in melted chocolate. *Makes 30.*

## One-stage treacle crisps

6 oz./175 g. plain flour

½ teaspoon cream of tartar

½ teaspoon bicarbonate of soda

¼ teaspoon salt

4 oz./100 g. luxury margarine

6 oz./175 g. castor sugar

3 tablespoons black treacle

2 oz./50 g. raisins, chopped

Sieve the flour, cream of tartar, bicarbonate of soda and salt into a mixing bowl. Place the remaining ingredients in the bowl and beat together with a wooden spoon until well mixed (approximately 2–3 minutes). Gather the mixture together with the fingertips and form into a roll.

**To freeze:** Cut the roll into four pieces and place dividing papers between them. Wrap the rolls in polythene tissue paper or aluminium foil. If wrapped in polythene tissue paper, seal before freezing.

**To prepare for cooking:** Unwrap and thaw at room temperature until the dough is soft enough to slice. Cut thinly and place the cookies fairly wide apart on a greased baking sheet. Bake in the centre of a moderately hot oven (375°F., 190°C., Gas Mark 5) for 7–10 minutes. Cool on a wire tray. *Makes 36–40.*

## Date and nut loaf

1 lb./450 g. plain flour

1 teaspoon salt

2 teaspoons baking powder

4 oz./100 g. butter or margarine

4 oz./100 g. soft brown sugar

6 oz./175 g. cooking dates, chopped

2 oz./50 g. walnuts, chopped

1 egg

scant ½ pint/5 dl. milk

Sieve the flour, salt and baking powder into a mixing bowl. Rub the butter into the flour, add the sugar, dates and walnuts. Make a well in the centre, add the egg and sufficient milk to make a soft dough. Turn the dough on to a floured board and knead lightly, shape into a roll and place in a greased 2-lb. (1-kg.) loaf tin. Bake in the centre of a moderately hot oven (375°F., 190°C., Gas Mark 5) for 50–60 minutes.

**To freeze:** Cool completely and wrap in polythene tissue paper, double or heavy duty foil or thick polythene. Seal and freeze.

**To prepare for serving:** Thaw, still wrapped, at room temperature allowing approximately 6 hours. *Makes a 2-lb. (1-kg.) loaf.*

## Banana fruit loaf

8 oz./225 g. self-raising flour

½ teaspoon salt

pinch mixed spice

2 oz./50 g. glacé cherries, washed and quartered

4 oz./100 g. castor sugar

1 heaped tablespoon golden syrup

2 oz./50 g. peel, chopped

2 oz./50 g. walnuts, coarsely chopped

4 oz./100 g. luxury margarine, sliced

1 lb./450 g. bananas, mashed

2 eggs

Sieve the flour, salt and spice into a mixing bowl. Dry the cherries and add to the bowl with the remaining ingredients then beat with a wooden spoon until evenly mixed. Spread in a 2-lb. (1-kg.) greased loaf tin, and bake in the centre of a moderate oven (350°F., 180°C., Gas Mark 4) for 1½–1¾ hours.

**To freeze:** Cool completely. Wrap in polythene tissue paper, a double thickness of foil, or thick polythene. Seal and freeze.

**To prepare for serving:** Thaw, still wrapped, at room temperature allowing approximately 6 hours. *Makes a 2-lb. (1-kg.) loaf.*

Gingerbread

## Gingerbread

4 oz./100 g. margarine

6 oz./175 g. black treacle

2 oz./50 g. golden syrup

¼ pint/1½ dl. milk

2 eggs

8 oz./225 g. plain flour

2 oz./50 g. brown sugar

1 rounded teaspoon mixed spice

1 teaspoon bicarbonate of soda

2 teaspoons ground ginger

4 oz./100 g. sultanas (optional)

Grease and line a 7-inch (18-cm.) square cake tin. Warm together the margarine, treacle and syrup. Add the milk and cool. Beat the eggs and blend with the mixture. Sieve the dry ingredients together, add the cooled mixture and blend with a tablespoon. Add the fruit if required. Turn into the prepared tin. Bake in the centre of a slow oven (300°F., 150°C., Gas Mark 2) for 1¼–1½ hours.

**To freeze:** Turn out of the tin and cool on a wire tray. Wrap in a polythene bag with all air excluded. Tightly seal and freeze.

**To prepare for serving:** Thaw, sealed, at room temperature for 4–6 hours. Top with water icing and chopped almonds. *Makes a 7-inch (18-cm.) square cake.*

## Plum cake ring

6 oz./175 g. butter or margarine

6 oz./175 g. soft brown sugar

3 large eggs

8 oz./225 g. self-raising flour

1 teaspoon baking powder

1 teaspoon mixed spice

8 oz./225 g. sultanas

6 oz./175 g. currants

4 oz./100 g. mixed cut peel

2 oz./50 g. glacé cherries

4 oz./100 g. walnuts, chopped

1 miniature bottle rum

*To decorate:*

crystallised fruits

castor sugar

Cream the butter and sugar until light and fluffy. Lightly whisk the eggs and beat into the butter and sugar mixture gradually. Sieve the flour, baking powder and mixed spice; fold into the creamed ingredients. Stir in the remaining ingredients and spoon the mixture into a greased and floured 3-pint (1¾-litre) ring mould. Or grease and flour the outside of a 1-lb. (454-g.) cocoa tin, weight it, and place centrally in a prepared 9-inch (23-cm.) cake tin. Bake in a hot oven (400°F., 200°C., Gas Mark 6) for 15 minutes then reduce the temperature to 300°F., 150°C., Gas Mark 2 for a further 2½–2¾ hours. Cool slightly before removing from the tin.

**To freeze:** Wrap tightly with polythene tissue paper and seal with freezer tape or wrap in a double thickness of foil. Store in a suitable container until frozen hard.

**To prepare for serving:** Thaw, wrapped, at room temperature. Pile crystallised fruits in the centre and sift with castor sugar. *Serves 18–20.*

# Scones

1 lb./450 g. plain flour

1 teaspoon salt

2 teaspoons bicarbonate of soda and

    4 teaspoons cream of tartar, or

    8 teaspoons baking powder

3 oz./75 g. castor sugar

3 oz./75 g. butter or margarine

2 eggs, plus sufficient milk to make $\frac{1}{2}$ pint/3 dl.

Sift the flour, salt, bicarbonate of soda and cream of tartar (or baking powder) together. Stir in the sugar. Rub in the fat. Beat the eggs and milk lightly together. Make a well in the centre of the flour mixture and pour the liquid into it. Stir lightly together to make a dough just firm enough to handle. Turn out on a floured board, roll or pat out by hand to $\frac{3}{8}$-inch ($\frac{3}{4}$-cm.) thickness. Cut into 2–2$\frac{1}{2}$-inch (5–6-cm.) rounds, bake on a floured baking sheet in a fairly hot oven (400°F., 200°C., Gas Mark 6) for 7–10 minutes. Cool.

**To freeze:** Pack into polythene bags or other suitable containers. Seal and freeze.

**To prepare for serving:** Thaw, covered, at room temperature for 2 hours. *Makes 16–20.*

# Chocolate cake

8 oz./225 g. self-raising flour

2 oz./50 g. cocoa powder

6 oz./175 g. castor sugar

$\frac{1}{2}$ teaspoon salt

4 oz./100 g. luxury margarine

$\frac{1}{4}$ pint plus 5 tablespoons/2 dl. milk

3 eggs

1$\frac{1}{2}$ tablespoons treacle

Grease an 8-inch (20-cm.) square or round cake tin. Line the bottom with greased paper. Sieve the dry ingredients into a large mixing bowl. Add the remaining ingredients and beat until well combined. Pour into the prepared tin. Bake slowly on the middle shelf of the oven at 300°F., 150°C., Gas Mark 2 for approximately 1$\frac{1}{4}$–1$\frac{1}{2}$ hours. Cool in the tin for 5 minutes then turn out.

**To freeze:** Cool and freeze in a polythene bag with all air excluded. Seal tightly and freeze.

**To prepare for serving:** Allow to thaw at room temperature for 4–6 hours. *Makes an 8-inch (20-cm.) square or round cake.*

# Feather sponge

5 oz./150 g. plain flour

1 oz./25 g. cornflour

2 teaspoons baking powder

$\frac{1}{2}$ teaspoon salt

5 oz./150 g. castor sugar

2 eggs, separated

6 tablespoons corn oil

6 tablespoons water

Line the bottom of two 7-inch (18-cm.) sandwich tins with greaseproof paper and grease lightly. Sieve the dry ingredients into a bowl. Mix together lightly with a fork the egg yolks, corn oil and water. Stir this into the dry ingredients. Whisk the egg whites until stiff, fold lightly into the mixture. Turn the mixture into the prepared tins. Bake in a moderately hot oven (375°F., 190°C., Gas Mark 5) for 25–30 minutes. Turn out and cool. Sandwich with jam.

**To freeze:** Wrap in a polythene bag with all the air excluded. Tightly seal and freeze.

**To prepare for serving:** Thaw, wrapped, at room temperature for 4–6 hours. *Makes a 7-inch (18-cm.) cake.*

# Lemon curd

2 lemons

8 oz./225 g. castor sugar

3 oz./75 g. butter

3 eggs

Finely grate the zest from the lemons and squeeze the juice. Place the juice, zest and sugar in a double boiler, or basin over hot water, and stir until the sugar has dissolved. Add the butter and allow to melt. Remove from the heat, cool and beat in the eggs. Return to the heat and stir constantly without boiling until smooth and thick.

**To freeze:** Cool and pack into plastic containers or wide-necked jars. Seal and freeze.

**To prepare for serving:** Thaw for 30 minutes at room temperature.

# Hostess menus

Dinner parties these days tend to be more the informal 'come in for an evening meal' type than the grand affairs they used to be. Since cooking has become a delightful hobby to so many people, a small dinner for four or six at the most gives many a dedicated cook the chance to display his or her talents to an appreciative audience. This makes it much more fun to give such a party, than if one looks on it purely as a social obligation.

There was a time when people were brought up to consider it vulgar to talk enthusiastically about food, or even notice what they were eating as a guest in someone else's home. Nowadays people will freely discuss the menu and compliment a hostess on her cooking as well as exchanging gastronomic reminiscences and treasured recipes. In fact, the subject of food will often take precedence over the traditional rather dull dinner party conversation.

My selection of menus and suitable dishes, therefore, avoids the more obvious choices, such as prawn cocktail, which figure in every hostess's repertoire. The quantities are for six people, and most of the dishes are unusual enough to make an agreeable talking point during the meal, and afterwards.

The three-course dinner is now generally accepted as suitable for even formal entertaining at home (your husband's wealthy relatives; his boss; in fact anyone you don't know well and would like to impress). But just because the freezer makes it so easy, I have included one four-course menu, in case you feel like serving a hot savoury, just for a change. Any of the other menus can be extended to four courses by serving a tempting cheese platter (some English and some foreign cheeses, please) or a beautiful bowl of fresh fruit as dessert if the meal has been rather a substantial one.

To impress your guests the fruit bowl should contain one rather unusual or expensive fruit. A pineapple as a centrepiece, for instance, looks extremely attractive, although at times these are quite cheap; Chinese gooseberries or lychees in their mysterious prickly brown overcoats are now sold in most large towns in season, or the gorgeous crimson or orange-skinned plums and nectarines which are now accepted arrivals on the midwinter scene. For the rest, add crisp, juicy apples, pears and oranges, and ripe but still firm bananas to round out the selection.

## Menus for special dinner parties

The following three menus are planned to give perfect balance to each meal. Reap the rewards of your labours and surprise your guests by serving luxury foods out of season.

**Menu 1**
Rich chicken liver pâté
Individual quiches
Apricot dessert

**Menu 2**
Gazpacho
Chicken with lemon cream
French apple pie

**Menu 3**
Silberbissen
Coquilles St. Jacques
Strawberries Romanoff
Délices de fromage

# MENU 1

## Rich chicken liver pâté

1 small onion, finely chopped

2 tablespoons corn oil

4–6 oz./100–175 g. fresh chicken livers

1 dessertspoon flour

1 hard-boiled egg yolk, mashed

6 oz./175 g. butter, softened

1 tablespoon sherry

2 tablespoons double cream

salt and pepper to taste

1 clove garlic, chopped (optional)

Fry the onion in the oil until golden, and remove from the pan. Trim the livers; wash, dry and coat in the flour. Put the livers in the pan, cover and cook gently for 5–6 minutes. When lightly cooked, chop roughly and pass them, with the onions, through a sieve. Add the hard-boiled egg yolk, butter, sherry, cream and seasoning. Mix together thoroughly until completely smooth and well blended or put into an electric blender.

**To freeze:** Pack in a foil pudding basin. Seal with a double thickness of foil and freeze.

**To prepare for serving:** Thaw at room temperature allowing 3–4 hours. Serve with toast. *Serves 6.*

## Individual quiches

6 oz./175 g. shortcrust pastry

1 tablespoon corn oil

1 small onion, finely chopped

2 rashers streaky bacon, finely chopped

1 egg yolk

½ pint/3 dl. milk

1 tablespoon parsley, chopped

½ teaspoon salt

pinch pepper

1 oz./25 g. cheese, grated

Roll out the pastry and line six 3-inch (7½-cm.) patty tins. Bake blind with baking beans in a fairly hot oven (400°F., 200°C., Gas Mark 6) for 5 minutes. Remove the baking beans and bake for a further 5 minutes. Heat the corn oil. Add the onion and bacon and fry without browning. Remove from the pan and drain.

Whisk the egg yolk and milk. Stir in the onion, bacon, parsley, salt, pepper and cheese. Divide the mixture between the six pastry cases. Bake in a moderately hot oven (375°F., 190°C., Gas Mark 5) for 15 minutes, or until the filling is set. Cool on a wire tray.

**To freeze:** When cold, freeze in a large plastic container until solid, then arrange in a plastic or foil container. Return to the freezer.

**To prepare for serving:** Thaw covered, at room temperature and, if liked, warm gently before serving. Garnish each quiche with a slice of tomato. *Serves 6.*

## Apricot dessert

1 lb./450 g. apricots

¼ pint/1½ dl. water

3 oz./75 g. castor sugar

little milk

1½ oz./40 g. cornflour

2 eggs, separated

¼ pint/1½ dl. single cream

1 dessertspoon apricot brandy (optional)

Halve and stone the apricots. Place in a saucepan with the water and sugar. Cover and cook slowly for 15 minutes or until tender. Rub the apricots through a sieve. Make up the purée to 1 pint (6 dl.) with milk. Blend the cornflour and egg yolks with a little of the purée. Heat the remainder. Stir in the blended cornflour and bring to the boil, stirring. Cook for a further 3 minutes, stirring all the time to prevent lumps from forming. Pour into a large mixing bowl and leave to cool. Stir in the cream and apricot brandy, if used. Whisk the egg whites until stiff and fold lightly into the apricot mixture. Pour into a dampened 1-lb. (450-g.) loaf tin and chill.

**To freeze:** Cover closely with double or heavy duty foil. Freeze.

**To prepare for serving:** Thaw, uncovered, at room temperature, allowing approximately 6 hours. Turn out of the tin and decorate with fresh fruit and whipped cream. *Serves 6.*

## MENU 2

### Gazpacho

$\frac{1}{4}$ pint/1$\frac{1}{2}$ dl. olive oil
3 cloves garlic, crushed
1 small onion, very finely chopped
1 teaspoon salt
5 tablespoons vinegar
1 large ripe avocado pear, peeled and stoned
1 15-oz./425-g. can tomatoes
1 15-oz./425-g. can tomato juice

Beat thoroughly with a rotary beater, or liquidise in a blender, the oil, garlic, onion, salt and vinegar. Dice the flesh from the avocado pear. Beat or liquidise the canned tomatoes, tomato juice and avocado pear. Press through a sieve. Blend the two mixtures together, in two batches if necessary.

**To freeze:** Pour into a polythene bag or plastic container. Seal, leaving a 1-inch (2$\frac{1}{2}$-cm.) headspace, and freeze.

**To prepare for serving:** Thaw overnight in the refrigerator or at room temperature until liquid but still chilled. Stir well and adjust seasoning. Serve sprinkled with fresh chopped parsley and chives. *Serves 6.*

### Chicken with lemon cream

1$\frac{1}{2}$ oz./40 g. butter
6 chicken breasts
2 tablespoons dry sherry
3 tablespoons dry white wine
grated zest of 1 lemon
1$\frac{1}{2}$ tablespoons lemon juice
salt and pepper to taste
$\frac{1}{4}$ pint/1$\frac{1}{2}$ dl. single cream
$\frac{1}{4}$ pint/1$\frac{1}{2}$ dl. double cream

Melt the butter in a frying pan, add the chicken pieces and fry until browned all over (approximately 5 minutes). Transfer the chicken to a shallow baking tin. Add the sherry, white wine, grated lemon zest, lemon juice and seasoning to taste to the juices in the pan. Stir well over gentle heat until thoroughly blended. Remove from the heat, add the cream, stir again and pour over the chicken.

**To freeze:** Cool rapidly, cover and seal the dish with a double thickness of foil before freezing.

**To prepare for serving:** Thaw at room temperature and transfer to an ovenproof serving dish. Sprinkle with 2 oz. (50 g.) grated Gruyère cheese, put in a moderate oven (350°F., 180°C., Gas Mark 4) for 35 minutes. Brown under the grill. Place a lemon butterfly on each portion, sprinkle with chopped parsley and serve with fluffy long-grain rice. *Serves 6.*

French apple tart

### French apple tart

1 oz./25 g. butter
1 teaspoon cinnamon
4 oz./100 g. soft brown sugar
4 large cooking apples
*For the pastry crust:*
5 oz./150 g. plain flour
$\frac{1}{2}$ teaspoon salt
4 oz./100 g. butter
1 egg, lightly beaten
2 tablespoons cold water

Butter a 9-inch (23-cm.) sandwich tin and line the bottom with a circle of buttered greaseproof paper. Sprinkle with cinnamon and brown sugar. Peel and core the apples and slice as thinly as

Butter a 9-inch (23-cm.) sandwich tin and line with greaseproof paper.

Sprinkle the base with cinnamon and brown sugar. Cover the bottom of the dish with concentric circles of apple slices.

Fill the tin with more layers of apple slices, well pressed down. Lightly press the circle of pastry on top.

Wrap in double or heavy duty foil and overwrap with polythene.

possible. Cover the bottom of the dish with concentric circles of apple slices, pressing them down firmly. Fill the tin with more layers of apple slices, well pressed down. Top with the rest of the butter.

Make the pastry crust, mixing the ingredients with a fork as the dough will be very soft. Chill before rolling out to make it easier to handle. Roll out to a circle large enough to fit the dish and press lightly on top.

**To freeze:** Wrap in a double thickness of foil or sheet polythene. Seal and freeze.

**To prepare for serving:** Put the pie in a very hot oven (450°F., 230°C., Gas Mark 8) while still frozen. Immediately reduce heat to 375°F., 190°C., Gas Mark 5. Bake for 30–35 minutes, remove from the oven and immediately invert on a serving dish and remove the greaseproof paper. Serve warm if liked with sweetened whipped cream. *Serves 6.*

# MENU 3
## Silberbissen

1 large grapefruit, halved

12 oz./350 g. cream cheese

3 tablespoons soured cream

1 tablespoon onion, finely chopped

salt and pepper to taste

1 tablespoon lemon juice

2 tablespoons walnut halves, chopped

Remove the grapefruit segments. Beat together the cream cheese, soured cream, onion, salt and pepper and lemon juice. Stir in lightly the grapefruit segments and chopped walnuts.

**To freeze:** Spoon into plastic containers. Seal, leaving a ½-inch (1-cm.) headspace, and freeze.

**To prepare for serving:** Thaw at room temperature and spoon into cocktail glasses lined with shredded lettuce. Serve with fingers of toast. *Serves 6.*

## Coquilles St. Jacques

$\frac{1}{4}$ pint/1$\frac{1}{2}$ dl. dry white vermouth or
   $\frac{1}{4}$ pint plus 4 tablespoons/2 dl. dry white wine
salt and pepper to taste
1 bay leaf
2 tablespoons finely chopped onion
1 lb./450 g. scallops
8 oz./225 g. mushrooms, sliced
1$\frac{1}{2}$ oz./40 g. butter
1$\frac{1}{2}$ oz./40 g. flour
$\frac{1}{4}$ pint/1$\frac{1}{2}$ dl. milk
2 egg yolks
$\frac{1}{4}$ pint/1$\frac{1}{2}$ dl. double cream
1 teaspoon lemon juice

Simmer together for 5 minutes the vermouth or wine, salt, pepper, bay leaf and onion. Add the scallops and sliced mushrooms. Add sufficient water just to cover, simmer covered for 5 minutes. Remove the scallops and mushrooms and boil the stock quickly to reduce to $\frac{1}{2}$ pint (3 dl.). Melt the butter, stir in the flour, blend in the stock and milk. Cook, stirring, for 1 minute. Remove from the heat. Blend the egg yolks with the cream, gradually stir the hot sauce into the egg and cream mixture. Return to the pan and reheat for 2 minutes but do not boil, stirring all the time. Season to taste with salt, pepper and lemon juice. Cut the scallops into bite-size pieces, stir with the mushrooms into the sauce. Butter six deep scallop shells, fill with the mixture.

**To freeze:** Cool rapidly. Cover closely with double or heavy duty foil and freeze.

**To prepare for serving:** Thaw in the refrigerator for about 4 hours, sprinkle with a little grated Gruyère cheese, dot with butter and grill for 15 minutes or until well browned. *Serves 6.*

## Strawberries Romanoff

1$\frac{1}{2}$ lb./675 g. frozen strawberries (sweetened)
$\frac{1}{4}$ pint/1$\frac{1}{2}$ dl. orange juice
7 tablespoons Curaçao or Cointreau
$\frac{1}{2}$ pint/3 dl. double cream
1 oz./25 g. icing sugar, sifted

Partially thaw the strawberries. Combine the orange juice and liqueur. Pour over the straw-

berries. Keep chilled. Place in a glass serving dish. Whip the cream and icing sugar and pile on top. *Serves 6.*

## Délices de fromage

4 slices streaky bacon, trimmed
3 oz./75 g. Gruyère cheese, grated
1 oz./25 g. Parmesan cheese, grated
1 small onion, grated
1 teaspoon mayonnaise
$\frac{1}{2}$ teaspoon dry mustard
6 large slices white bread

Grill the bacon until crisp and crush finely. Mix the grated cheese, onion and bacon with the mayonnaise and mustard. Toast the bread on one side. Trim, halve, spread the mixture on the un-toasted side.

**To freeze:** Stack on a double thickness of foil, dividing each slice with foil. Wrap, seal and freeze.

**To prepare for serving:** Thaw, wrapped, at room temperature. Unwrap, then grill, cheese side up, until golden. *Serves 6.*

# MORE PARTY DISHES
## Consommé

8-12 oz./225–350 g. shin of beef
2 carrots, sliced
1 leek, sliced
1 stick celery, sliced
2 pints/generous litre brown stock
4 stalks parsley
1 sprig thyme
$\frac{1}{2}$ bay leaf
3–4 egg whites, lightly whisked

Trim the fat from the meat and cut into fine strips. Put it into a saucepan with the vegetables and stock. Tie the parsley stalks, thyme and bay leaf with thread and add to the ingredients in the pan, together with the egg whites. Bring slowly to simmering point, stirring all the time. When the liquid begins to cloud, stop stirring and continue to simmer gently for 10–15 minutes, or until the egg has hardened and the consommé is clear and brilliant. Put a clean, wet cloth over a large mixing bowl and ladle the consommé through it. Do not press the soup through the cloth. Discard the meat and vegetables.

**To freeze:** Pack in plastic containers. Seal and freeze.

**To prepare for serving:** Immerse the container in hot water. Gently reheat the contents in a saucepan. Add 3 tablespoons dry sherry and correct the seasoning before serving. *Serves 6.*

## French onion soup

1 oz./25 g. margarine
1 lb./450 g. onions, skinned and sliced
1½ pints/scant litre stock or 2 stock cubes and water
salt to taste
1 oz./25 g. cornflour
¼ pint/1½ dl. cold water

Melt the margarine in a pan. Add the sliced onions, cover and cook gently for 20–30 minutes until soft but not coloured. Remove the lid and allow to cook until brown. Stir in the stock and salt, re-cover and simmer for 30 minutes. Blend the cornflour and water together, stir into the soup. Continue to cook, stirring, until thick.

**To freeze:** Cool and pour into plastic or other suitable containers. Seal and freeze.

**To prepare for serving:** Gently reheat in a pan. Ladle into soup plates. Serve with slices of toasted French bread and grated Parmesan cheese. *Serves 6.*

## Cream of cucumber soup

2 young cucumbers
1 oz./25 g. butter
salt and pepper to taste
pinch sugar
¼ pint/1½ dl. chicken stock
¼ pint/1½ dl. white sauce
green colouring

Wipe and peel the cucumbers, slice in half lengthways, remove the seeds. Cut into thick slices, blanch in boiling water for 30 seconds and drain.

Melt the butter in a heavy saucepan, add the cucumbers, seasoning and sugar. Cover and cook gently until soft. Add the chicken stock and white sauce. Bring to the boil. Pass through a fine sieve, or liquidise in a blender, and return to the saucepan. Thin down with a little more stock if necessary. Check the seasoning and add a little green colouring.

**To freeze:** Cool and pack into a plastic container, leaving a 1-inch (2½-cm.) headspace.

**To prepare for serving:** Immerse the container in hot water to loosen the contents. Reheat gently in a saucepan. Add a 2½-oz. (71-g.) carton single cream and reheat without boiling. *Serves 6.*

## Vichyssoise

6 large leeks
4 medium potatoes
2 oz./50 g. butter
1½ pints/scant litre chicken stock or
    2 stock cubes and water
salt and pepper to taste
*To garnish:*
1 heaped tablespoon chopped chives

Trim all green parts from the leeks, wash thoroughly and cut into short lengths. Peel and slice the potatoes. Heat the butter in a saucepan and sauté the leeks gently until soft but not coloured, then add the potatoes, chicken stock and seasoning and simmer until the vegetables are tender. Press through a fine sieve or liquidise in an electric blender.

**To freeze:** Pack in plastic containers, leaving a 1-inch (2½-cm.) headspace. Cover and freeze.

**To prepare for serving:** Thaw at room temperature, stir in ¼ pint (1½ dl.) fresh or soured cream. Sprinkle each serving with chopped chives. *Serves 6.*

## Piquant avocado dip

2 medium avocados
2 tablespoons lemon juice
6 oz./175 g. cream cheese
1 teaspoon salt
¼ teaspoon pepper
dash Tabasco sauce
1 tablespoon finely grated onion

Stone the avocados and mash or sieve the flesh until smooth. Add the remaining ingredients and mix well.

**To freeze:** Pack into a suitable plastic container. Seal and label.

**To prepare for serving:** De-frost in the refrigerator overnight, stir thoroughly and serve chilled. If required quickly, hold the container under warm water until the dip can be broken up and mixed with a fork until smooth. Garnish with lemon and sprigs of parsley. Serve with potato crisps and small savoury biscuits. *Serves 6.*

Terrine of pork

## Terrine of pork

1 lb./450 g. lean pork, minced
8 oz./225 g. pork sausage meat
4 oz./100 g. rolled oats
rind and juice of ½ lemon
salt and pepper to taste
½ teaspoon sage
1 onion, grated
1 egg, beaten
6 oz./175 g. streaky bacon rashers

Mix together all the ingredients except the rashers. De-rind the rashers and place on a board, then stretch them by stroking lengthways gently, using a dinner knife. Arrange in a 2-lb. (1-kg.) loaf tin. Carefully press the meat mixture into the tin and level off the top. Cover with foil and put in a baking tin of water. Cook for 1½ hours in a moderate oven (350°F., 180°C., Gas Mark 4). When cooked, place a weight on top and leave overnight.

**To freeze:** Ease the pâté out of the loaf tin. Cut into 12 slices. Put polythene tissue paper or foil dividers between every slice; wrap closely in double or heavy duty foil. Freeze.

**To prepare for serving:** Open the package and spread out the portions. Thaw at room temperature for about 1 hour. *Serves 6.*

Glazed salmon trout

## Glazed salmon trout

1 2½–3-lb./1–1¼-kg. salmon trout, thawed
6 parsley stalks
½ lemon, cut into thick slices
*To garnish:*
2 tablespoons powdered gelatine, soaked in
   2 tablespoons water
2 pints/generous litre water
juice of ½ lemon
stuffed olives, sliced
1 canned red pimento, sliced
slices of lemon

Wrap the fish in a well sealed foil parcel with the parsley stalks and lemon. Place on a baking sheet and cook in the centre of a moderate oven (350°F., 180°C., Gas Mark 4) allowing 20 minutes per lb.

(450 g.). Unwrap and cool on a wire tray.

To garnish, heat a little of the water and pour on to the soaked gelatine; stir to dissolve before adding to the rest of the water with the lemon juice. Leave in a cool place until on the point of setting. Put a clean tray under the wire rack and spoon the jelly over the fish. Decorate with the olives and pimento. Pour the remaining jelly into an oblong tin and allow to set. Turn out of the tin, dice and arrange on the base of the serving dish. Transfer the fish to the serving dish and garnish with lemon slices. *Serves 6–8.*

Rice with mushrooms and scampi

## Rice with mushrooms and scampi

8 oz./225 g. button mushrooms

10 oz./275 g. long-grain rice

3 oz./75 g. butter

12 oz./350 g. frozen scampi, thawed

1 tablespoon brandy

1 tablespoon tomato purée

2 tablespoons flour

$\frac{1}{4}$ pint/1 $\frac{1}{2}$ dl. milk

2 tablespoons oil

salt and pepper

3 tablespoons grated Parmesan cheese

Wash and dry the mushrooms. Cook the rice in boiling salted water until tender (from 14–20 minutes depending on the type used). In a saucepan heat 1 oz. (25 g.) of the butter, add the scampi and cook for 2 minutes. Add the brandy and when evaporated stir in the tomato purée and flour. Add the milk, stir and cook for another minute. Cover and simmer gently for 10 minutes. Meanwhile, in another pan, heat 1 oz. (25 g.) butter with 1 tablespoon oil and sauté the mushrooms gently for 3$\frac{1}{2}$ minutes; season with salt and pepper. When the rice is cooked, drain thoroughly and return to the saucepan with the remaining butter and the cheese. Heat gently until the butter and cheese combine with the rice.

**To freeze:** Cool the rice and pack separately in a foil pudding basin. Cover with double or heavy duty foil and freeze. Pack the scampi mixture into a carton. Seal and freeze.

**To prepare for serving:** Thaw at room temperature allowing approximately 4–5 hours. Put the rice in a sieve or colander and place over a saucepan of boiling water. Cover and heat through. Add a lightly beaten egg yolk and $\frac{1}{4}$ pint (1$\frac{1}{2}$ dl.) single cream to the scampi mixture. Reheat in a saucepan. Do not allow to boil. *Serves 6.*

## Prawn curry

3 pints/1$\frac{3}{4}$ litres fresh prawns or

   1 8-oz./226-g. packet frozen prawns

2 tablespoons corn oil

2 medium onions, chopped

3 tablespoons cornflour

2 chicken stock cubes

3 teaspoons curry paste

$\frac{1}{2}$ teaspoon salt

1$\frac{1}{2}$ tablespoons demerara sugar

1 14-oz./396-g. can tomatoes

1 bay leaf

1 pint/6 dl. water

Peel the prawns and remove the veins. (If using frozen prawns, de-frost.) Heat the corn oil. Add the onion and fry until soft without browning. Add the cornflour, stock cubes, curry paste, salt, sugar, tomatoes and bay leaf. Stir in the water and bring to the boil, stirring. Cover and simmer for 30 minutes. Add the prawns and simmer for a further 20 minutes.

**To freeze:** Cool, put into a suitable container, cover and seal before freezing.

**To prepare for serving:** Turn carefully into a saucepan and reheat over gentle heat. Serve with plain boiled rice. *Serves 6.*

## Boeuf à la bourguignonne

2 lb./900 g. best stewing steak

2 tablespoons flour

salt and pepper

1½ oz./40 g. dripping or lard

4 oz./100 g. streaky bacon, diced

12 small onions or shallots

1 clove garlic, crushed

pinch thyme

½ bay leaf

1 15-oz./425-g. can cream of mushroom soup

2 oz./50 g. mushrooms, sliced

¼ pint/1½ dl. Burgundy

Boeuf à la bourguignonne

Trim the meat and cut into neat 1-inch (2½-cm.) squares, toss in the seasoned flour and fry in hot fat in a flameproof casserole for a few minutes to seal. Remove the meat from the casserole and keep hot. Fry the bacon, and return the meat to the casserole. Add six onions, the garlic, thyme, bay leaf, mushroom soup, mushrooms and Burgundy. Cook for 1½ hours in a warm oven (325°F., 170°C., Gas Mark 3). Add the remaining onions.

**To freeze:** Remove the bay leaf and cool rapidly. Pack in plastic or foil containers. Seal and freeze.

**To prepare for serving:** Thaw at room temperature allowing approximately 6 hours for thawing. Cook for 40 minutes in a warm oven (325°F., 170°C., Gas Mark 3). *Serves 6.*

## Boeuf à la provençale

2 lb./900 g. chuck or buttock steak

4 oz./100 g. belly of pork

1 tablespoon olive oil

1 11-oz./312-g. can tomatoes

¼ pint/1½ dl. stock or water

6 parsley stalks and ½ bay leaf, tied with thread to make
   a bouquet garni

½ teaspoon salt

pinch pepper

½ teaspoon rosemary

¼ pint/1½ dl. dry white wine

6 green olives, stoned

Trim the beef and cut into 1-inch (2½-cm.) cubes. Trim the pork and dice finely. Heat the oil in a

large saucepan and add the pork; fry until the fat is rendered down. Add the beef to the pork and fry briskly to brown on all sides. Add the tomatoes, with the juice, the stock, bouquet garni, salt, pepper and rosemary. Cover with a lid and simmer very gently for 1 hour. Add the wine and continue to cook for a further 15 minutes.

**To freeze:** Add the olives and cool. Put into a plastic, foil or other suitable container, cover closely and seal before freezing.

**To prepare for serving:** Turn into a saucepan, adjust the seasoning and thicken with 1 oz. (25 g.) beurre manié. *Serves 6.*

**Beurre manié:** Work butter and flour together, using one-and-a-half parts of butter to one part flour. This can be made in bulk and stored in the refrigerator for up to 6 weeks or it can be stored in the freezer for up to 3 months. Weigh the required amount and stir into soups or stews to thicken.

## Rich beef casserole

2 lb./900 g. chuck or buttock steak

1 oz./25 g. seasoned flour

2 tablespoons cooking oil

1 large onion, finely chopped

1 clove garlic

1 teaspoon salt

1 tablespoon tomato purée

1 teaspoon sugar

½ teaspoon dried basil

pinch pepper

½ pint/3 dl. stock or water

¼ pint/1½ dl. dry red wine

Cut the meat into 1-inch (2½-cm.) cubes and toss in the seasoned flour. Heat the oil in a large saucepan and when it is very hot, fry the meat to brown on all sides. Lower the heat and add the onion. Crush the garlic with the salt and add it to the ingredients in the pan. Continue to cook until the onion softens. Mix in the tomato purée and add the sugar, basil, pepper and stock. Cover with a lid and simmer over a gentle heat for 45 minutes before adding the wine; cook for a further 30 minutes.

**To freeze:** Cool rapidly, put into a suitable plastic container, cover closely and seal before freezing.

**To prepare for serving:** Turn into a saucepan and reheat gently. *Serves 6.*

Boeuf stroganoff

## Boeuf stroganoff

3 tablespoons cooking oil or 2 oz./50 g. butter

1 onion, peeled and sliced

1 small clove garlic, crushed

1¼ lb./575 g. stewing steak, cut into thin strips
    1½ inches/3½ cm. long

4 oz./100 g. mushrooms, sliced

pinch paprika

2 teaspoons Worcestershire sauce

1 packet tomato soup

¾ pint/4 dl. water

Melt the oil or butter in a saucepan and add the onion, garlic and meat. Cover, and simmer gently for 30 minutes. Add the mushrooms, paprika, Worcestershire sauce and contents of the packet of tomato soup. Gradually stir in the water, bring to the boil, cover and simmer for 30 minutes or until the meat is tender.

**To freeze:** Cool and spoon into a foil or plastic container. Seal and freeze.

**To prepare for serving:** Heat in a warm oven (325°F., 170°C., Gas Mark 3) and add ¼ pint (1½ dl.) yogurt or soured cream when the beef is hot but not bubbling. *Serves 6.*

## Rich beef stew with mustard croûtons

1½ lb./675 g. stewing steak

1 tablespoon corn oil

1 large onion

salt and pepper to taste

1 tablespoon French mustard

1 beef stock cube

2 oz./50 g. raisins

¾ pint/4 dl. light ale

½ oz./15 g. cornflour

*For the mustard croûtons:*

2 slices stale white bread

1 teaspoon dry mustard

oil for frying

chopped parsley to garnish

Cut the meat into even-sized dice. Heat the corn oil in a flameproof casserole and sauté the peeled and chopped onion and meat in it until brown. Add salt and pepper to taste, the French mustard, stock cube and raisins. Stir in the ale, bring to the boil, cover and simmer gently until the meat is tender, about 1½ hours. Moisten the cornflour with a little cold water, stir into the casserole, bring to the boil stirring all the time. Cook for a further 3 minutes. To make the croûtons, cut the bread into small triangles. Place in a shallow bowl and sift mustard over them through a sieve, shaking the bowl gently to coat the bread. Fry in very hot oil until golden brown on both sides. Drain well.

**To freeze:** Cool rapidly and pack the stew and croûtons separately in plastic containers.

**To prepare for serving:** Turn the stew into a saucepan and reheat gently. Garnish with croûtons, thawed at room temperature and sprinkled with parsley. *Serves 4.*

## Sauté de veau Marengo

2 lb./900 g. shoulder of veal

2 oz./50 g. butter

2 tablespoons oil

2 medium onions, peeled and chopped

1 tablespoon flour

$\frac{1}{4}$ pint/1$\frac{1}{2}$ dl. dry white wine

1 tablespoon tomato purée

$\frac{1}{2}$ bay leaf, tied together with 4 parsley stalks and
   1 sprig thyme

$\frac{1}{4}$ teaspoon basil

salt and pepper

$\frac{1}{2}$ teaspoon sugar

8 oz./225 g. button mushrooms, washed and trimmed

Cut the meat into 2-inch (5-cm.) cubes. Heat the butter and oil together in a large heavy frying pan; add the meat to the pan and brown over a brisk heat. Remove the meat and sauté the onions until soft but not coloured. Sprinkle the flour over the onions and cook gently for 1 minute. Transfer the onion to a saucepan and add the meat to it. Pour the wine over the meat; add the tomato purée, bouquet garni, basil, salt, pepper and sugar. Cover the saucepan with greaseproof paper and a tight-fitting lid. Simmer for 1 hour. Halve the mushrooms and add to the saucepan. Continue to cook for 3 minutes.

**To freeze:** Cool rapidly and spoon into plastic or other suitable containers, leaving a $\frac{1}{2}$-inch (1-cm.) headspace. Seal and freeze.

**To prepare for serving:** Thaw at room temperature for about 6 hours. Reheat in a saucepan. Garnish with triangles of fried bread before serving. *Serves 6.*

58

Gingered pork curry

## Gingered pork curry

8 oz./225 g. desiccated coconut

1 pint/6 dl. boiling water

4 oz./100 g. butter

2 onions, peeled and chopped

2 green peppers, chopped

2 sticks celery, chopped

3 lb./1$\frac{1}{4}$ kg. bladebone of pork, cubed

2 tablespoons flour

2–3 tablespoons curry powder

1 teaspoon ground ginger

2 tablespoons soy sauce

2 cooking apples, peeled and chopped

salt to taste

Place the coconut in a basin and pour over the boiling water. Allow to stand for at least 2 hours (overnight if possible) then strain off the 'milk' and squeeze the coconut to get out as much liquid as possible. Melt the butter and fry the onion, chopped pepper and celery until the vegetables are softened. Add the meat and toss over high heat until sealed. Sprinkle over the flour, curry powder and ginger, stir well and allow to cook for about 3 minutes. Gradually add the soy sauce, coconut milk and apple and bring to the boil, stirring constantly. Add a little extra water if too thick. Cover, simmer for 20 minutes and add salt if desired.

**To freeze:** Divide the curry between eight boilable bags if individual portions are required, or pack in larger quantities, press out excess air. Seal and freeze.

**To prepare for serving:** Place the required number of bags, still frozen, in a pan of boiling water and reheat for 15–25 minutes, depending on quantity of contents. Serve with fluffy boiled rice. (Portions of cooked rice can be frozen in boiling bags to be reheated in the same way as the curry.) *Serves 8.*

## Pork satay with golden and white rice

2 lb./900 g. pork fillet
3 tablespoons peanut butter
1 teaspoon ground coriander
1 large onion, finely grated
1 teaspoon salt
1 tablespoon brown sugar
2 tablespoons lemon juice
1 tablespoon soy sauce
1 teaspoon Tabasco sauce
pinch ground ginger

Cut up the pork fillet into 1-inch (2½-cm.) cubes. Leave overnight in the refrigerator in a marinade made by mixing the remaining ingredients well together.

**To freeze:** Pack meat and marinade in container, seal, label.

**To prepare for serving:** De-frost, drain and reserve the marinade. Thread the meat, pieces of onion and a few bay leaves, if liked, on skewers or spread on foil in the grill pan. Grill under high heat for 5 minutes. Turn, brush with the marinade and grill for a further 5 minutes. Reduce the heat and continue basting and turning for 20 minutes, or until the meat is tender. Serve with golden and white rice. *Serves 6.*

## Golden and white rice

Cook 4 oz. (100 g.) long-grain rice in boiling salted water. Cook a similar amount of rice in another pan, together with a few saffron strands (or a pinch of powdered saffron) and ½ teaspoon turmeric. Refresh the white rice, shake dry and turn on to a serving dish. Refresh the golden rice, place on top of the white rice. Dissolve 1 oz. (25 g.) sugar in 2 fluid oz. (50 ml.) orange juice. Add 1 tablespoon very thin slivers of orange peel and boil in the syrup for 1 minute. Pour over the rice. *Serves 6.*

## Stuffed fillet of pork

1 lb./450 g. pork fillet (tenderloin)
2 oz./50 g. butter or margarine
1 medium onion, peeled and finely chopped
4 oz./100 g. mushrooms, thinly sliced
1 oz./25 g. flour
½ pint/3 dl. chicken stock
pinch pepper
½ teaspoon salt
*For the filling:*
1 small onion, peeled and finely chopped
8 oz./225 g. streaky bacon, cooked and diced
3 tablespoons breadcrumbs
4 oz./100 g. sausage meat
¼ teaspoon salt
¼ teaspoon mixed herbs
1 egg, beaten

Trim the pork and cut into six pieces. Beat each piece between two sheets of wet greaseproof paper until very thin. Combine all the ingredients for the filling and spread equal portions on to each piece of pork. Fold the opposite sides to overlap, then tuck the ends over, parcel-fashion. Secure with cocktail sticks.

Melt the butter in a saucepan and cook the pork briskly until brown on all sides. Remove from the pan. Add the onion and mushrooms to the pan and cook gently until soft, but not coloured. Return the pork to the pan, add the flour, liquid and seasoning. Cover with a tight-fitting lid and simmer for 15 minutes.

**To freeze:** Cool rapidly. Pack into plastic or other suitable containers, leaving a ½-inch (1-cm.) headspace. Seal and freeze.

**To prepare for serving:** Immerse the container in hot water. Gently reheat in a saucepan. Serve with plain boiled rice. *Serves 6.*

## New Zealand guard of honour

2 best ends of neck of lamb, 6 bones each, de-frosted
few cutlet frills
glacé cherries

This is a very professional looking roast, very easy to cook and serve. The two best ends of neck must each have the same number of cutlets, five, six or seven. Remove the chine bone from each joint, trim and clean the bone tips of $1\frac{1}{2}$ inches ($3\frac{1}{2}$ cm.) of fat. Place the two joints together in a roasting pan, pressing the bones together to cross in the centre and protrude at each side. Pad the bone tips and roast in a well greased roasting pan in a moderately hot oven (375°F., 190°C., Gas Mark 5) for 1 hour. To serve, top the bone tips with cutlet frills and glacé cherries; garnish with parsley and serve with roast potatoes. *Serves 6.*

## Sautéed sweetbreads

$1\frac{1}{2}$ lb./675 g. sweetbreads
$\frac{3}{4}$ pint/4 dl. chicken stock or 1 stock cube and water
$1\frac{1}{2}$ oz./40 g. seasoned flour
beaten egg and breadcrumbs for coating

Soak the sweetbreads in salted, cold water for 1 hour. Drain and rinse. Put the sweetbreads in a saucepan, cover with water and bring to the boil. Drain and cool. Remove any fat. Simmer in the stock for 25 minutes or until tender. Drain, cool and cut into bite-size pieces. Toss in seasoned flour, dip in egg and coat with breadcrumbs.

**To freeze:** Pack in a polythene bag. Seal tightly and freeze.

**To prepare for serving:** Thaw, covered, in the refrigerator overnight. Fry in butter and serve with tomato sauce. *Serves 6.*

## Chicken with pineapple

2 oz./50 g. butter or margarine
1 small green pepper, de-seeded and sliced
2 oz./50 g. flour
$\frac{1}{2}$ pint/3 dl. milk
$\frac{1}{2}$ pint/3 dl. chicken stock
$1\frac{1}{2}$ lb./675 g. cooked chicken, diced
1 12-oz./340-g. can pineapple cubes, drained
salt and pepper to taste

Heat the butter and fry the sliced pepper gently for 5 minutes. Set aside and stir the flour into the butter. Combine the milk and chicken stock and gradually add to the flour and butter. Stir over a moderate heat until the sauce is smooth and thick. Add the green pepper, chicken, pineapple, salt and pepper and a little of the fruit juice if liked.

**To freeze:** Cool quickly. Pack into polythene or other suitable containers, leaving a $\frac{1}{2}$-inch (1-cm.) headspace.

**To prepare for serving:** Turn into a double boiler and heat through, for approximately 30 minutes. *Serves 6.*

## Chicken paprika

1 3-lb./$1\frac{1}{4}$-kg. chicken
seasoned cornflour for coating
2 tablespoons corn oil
1 onion, sliced
1 chicken stock cube
1 10-oz./283-g. can tomatoes, drained
1 green pepper, sliced
$\frac{1}{4}$ teaspoon garlic salt
1 tablespoon paprika pepper
$\frac{1}{2}$ pint/3 dl. water

Joint the chicken and coat with seasoned corn-flour. Heat the corn oil in a large saucepan and brown the chicken pieces on both sides. Remove from the pan. Add the onion to the pan and cook until tender. Add the chicken stock cube, tomatoes, pepper, garlic salt and paprika pepper. Stir in the water. Return the chicken to the pan, cover and simmer gently for 40–50 minutes or until the chicken is tender. Remove the chicken joints and boil the sauce in the pan rapidly until it is reduced by half.

**To freeze:** Cool rapidly, put into a suitable container, cover closely and seal before freezing.

**To prepare for serving:** Turn into a saucepan and reheat gently. Plain boil 12 oz. (350 g.) Patna rice and put it around the edge of the serving dish. Place the chicken joints in the centre. Add $\frac{1}{4}$ pint ($1\frac{1}{2}$ dl.) soured cream to sauce and reheat without boiling. Pour over the chicken. *Serves 6.*

# Chicken chop suey

1 large head celery

3 large onions

salt and pepper to taste

1 tablespoon sugar

2 pints/generous litre chicken stock or
    2 stock cubes and water

1 can bean sprouts

1 can bamboo shoots

1 lb./450 g. cooked chicken, cut into fine strips

1½ oz./40 g. cornflour

3 tablespoons cold water

2 tablespoons soy sauce

Clean the celery and cut into thin strips. Peel and finely slice the onions. Simmer the celery, onion, salt, pepper and sugar in the stock and the liquid from the cans of bean sprouts and bamboo shoots for 20 minutes. Add the chicken, bean sprouts and finely chopped bamboo shoots to the vegetable mixture. Blend the cornflour with the cold water and stir into the mixture. Simmer gently for 10 minutes, stirring frequently. Add the soy sauce.

**To freeze:** Cool rapidly, pack in a large plastic container. Seal and freeze.

**To prepare for serving:** Thaw at room temperature allowing approximately 6 hours. Reheat gently in a covered saucepan.    *Serves 6.*

# Poulet sauté Grand Monarque

1 oz./25 g. butter

1 tablespoon cooking oil

6 chicken pieces

1 medium onion, peeled and finely chopped

6 button onions, peeled

6 button mushrooms, washed and trimmed

3 tablespoons brandy

¼ teaspoon tarragon

¼ pint/1½ dl. stock or water

½ teaspoon salt

¼ pint/1½ dl. dry white wine

Heat the butter and oil in a large frying pan. When very hot add the chicken pieces and fry to brown on all sides. Transfer the chicken to an ovenproof dish. Lower the heat and sauté the chopped onion until soft but not brown; add the button onions and cook until golden. Spoon the onions into the dish with the chicken. Fry the mushrooms gently for 2 minutes; set aside.

Pour the brandy over the chicken and set alight. When the flames have died down add the remaining ingredients, with the exception of the wine. Cover with a lid and cook in the centre of a moderate oven (350°F., 180°C., Gas Mark 4) for 45 minutes. Add the wine and continue to cook for a further 15 minutes.

**To freeze:** Add the mushrooms and cool rapidly. Put into a suitable container, cover closely and seal before freezing.

**To prepare for serving:** Turn into a saucepan and reheat gently. Correct the seasoning and thicken with 1 oz. (25 g.) beurre manié (see page 56). Lower the heat and simmer for 10–12 minutes.    *Serves 6.*

# Jugged hare

1 hare, skinned and jointed (reserve blood)

salt and pepper to taste

bouquet garni

2 stock cubes (optional)

seasoned flour

8 oz./225 g. streaky bacon, diced

3 carrots, peeled and sliced

1 large onion, stuck with 6 cloves

sprig thyme

pinch mace

salt and pepper

¼ pint/1½ dl. red wine

4 oz./100 g. redcurrant jelly

Use the carcass and head of the hare to make stock, seasoning well with salt, pepper and a bouquet garni, or use 2 beef stock cubes to 1¼ pints (7 dl.) boiling water.

Turn the joints in seasoned flour. Fry the bacon gently and set aside, retaining the dripping. Fry the joints of hare in the rendered fat in a saucepan or flameproof casserole to seal all surfaces. Add to the bacon with the carrots, onion, herbs and seasoning.

Pour in enough stock just to cover, put on the

lid, and simmer gently for 2–2½ hours according to the size and age of the hare. Ten minutes before it is ready, mix together the blood, red wine and redcurrant jelly and add to the hare, to thicken the sauce.

**To freeze:** Remove the joints and reduce the sauce slightly, if desired, by further simmering. Cool rapidly; either freeze in the casserole or put into some other suitable container. Cover closely and seal before freezing.

**To prepare for serving:** Turn into a saucepan, reheat carefully over gentle heat.    *Serves 6.*

## Casserole of pigeons

4 oz./100 g. pork
4 oz./100 g. veal
3 wood pigeons, cleaned
4 oz./100 g. streaky bacon, stretched
1 oz./25 g. seasoned flour
2 oz./50 g. butter
½ pint/3 dl. chicken stock (see page 29)
1 onion
1 carrot
6 parsley stalks
salt and pepper to taste
8 oz./225 g. mushrooms

Finely mince the pork and the veal together. Divide the mixture into three and put a portion in the body cavity of each bird. Cover the breasts with bacon and secure with string. Coat the birds with seasoned flour, melt 1 oz. (25 g.) of the butter in the casserole and brown the birds on all sides over a brisk heat. Add the stock, onion, carrot, parsley stalks and seasoning. Cover with a lid and bake in the centre of a moderate oven (325°F., 170°C., Gas Mark 3) for 2–2½ hours.

Remove the pigeons from the casserole dish; remove the bacon, cut into dice and set aside. Cut the pigeons in half down the centre. Melt the remaining butter in a small saucepan, add the mushrooms and cook for 1½ minutes.

**To freeze:** Put the pigeons into a small baking tin with the bacon, mushrooms and strained liquor. Cool rapidly. Cover and seal with foil before freezing.

**To prepare for serving:** Partially thaw at room temperature allowing approximately 2 hours. Reheat in a moderate oven (350°F., 180°C., Gas Mark 4).    *Serves 6.*

## Baked Alaska

1 8-inch/20-cm. sponge cake
1 tablespoon raspberry jam
1 family brick ice cream

Spread the base of the cake with the jam. Mash the ice cream with a fork and spread on top of the jam.

**To freeze:** Place on a baking sheet and freeze until firm, then wrap with foil.

**To prepare for serving:** Whisk 2 egg whites stiffly and gradually add 3 oz. (75 g.) castor sugar whilst still whisking. When the meringue is stiff and shiny, remove the base from the freezer, unwrap and spoon the meringue on top. Cook in the top of a pre-heated very hot oven (450°F., 230°C., Gas Mark 8) for 3–5 minutes or until brown. Serve immediately.    *Serves 6.*

## Rum sponge

3 eggs
6 oz./175 g. castor sugar
3 oz./75 g. plain flour
¼ pint/1½ dl. water
2 tablespoons rum

Put the eggs and half the sugar in a mixing bowl over a saucepan of hot water. Whisk until the mixture is thick enough to leave a trail. Sieve the flour on to the surface of the mixture and carefully fold it in.

Pour into a greased 8-inch (20-cm.) savarin tin and bake in the centre of a moderately hot oven (375°F., 190°C., Gas Mark 5) for 30–35 minutes or until firm to the touch and golden brown in colour. Turn out and cool on a wire tray.

Dissolve the remaining sugar in the water. Bring to the boil and continue to boil rapidly for 7 minutes; add the rum. Cool, then prick holes in the sponge with a skewer. Brush with the rum-flavoured syrup until it is all absorbed into the cake.

**To freeze:** Wrap tightly in double or heavy duty foil, polythene tissue paper or thick polythene. Seal and freeze.

**To prepare for serving:** Thaw, covered, at room temperature allowing approximately 8 hours. Unwrap and place on a serving dish. Top with peeled and quartered pears frozen in syrup. Use for decoration orange segments and glacé cherries. *Serves 6–8.*

## Frozen mocha sponge pudding

1 4-oz./113-g. packet chocolate chips
4 tablespoons strong coffee
2 sponge cakes, baked in 7- by 11-inch/18- by 28-cm.
   Swiss roll tins
8 oz./225 g. unsalted butter
1 lb./450 g. icing sugar, sieved
2 egg yolks

Soften the chocolate in a basin, over a saucepan of hot water. When melted, gradually add the coffee. Trim the edges of both sponges and cut them across the width. Cream the butter until soft, then gradually work in the icing sugar and egg yolks. Beat the chocolate into the mixture.

Spread one piece of sponge with one-third of the chocolate filling, then build up the layers pressing each piece of sponge firmly in place on top of the filling. Finish with a sponge layer.

**To freeze:** Fit into a rectangular cake tin or container until frozen, then wrap in double or heavy duty foil and replace in the freezer.

**To prepare for serving:** Thaw wrapped at room temperature, for 4–5 hours. Sieve icing sugar over the top. *Serves 6.*

## Lemon chiffon pie

1 lemon
2 eggs, separated
2 oz./50 g. castor sugar
2 teaspoons gelatine dissolved in
   2 tablespoons hot water
1 baked 9-inch/23-cm. flan case

Squeeze the lemon juice into a mixing bowl and add half the zest, finely grated. Add the egg yolks and sugar and beat, over a saucepan of hot water,

until light and fluffy. Remove from the heat and continue to whisk until cool. Whisk the egg whites stiffly. Whisk the gelatine into the egg yolk mixture and continue to whisk until it is on setting point. Quickly fold in the egg whites; turn the mixture into the flan case and chill until set. Partly freeze.

**To freeze:** Cover the filling with polythene tissue and wrap the pie in double or heavy duty foil to seal before returning to the freezer.

**To prepare for serving:** Thaw in wrapping, at room temperature, for 4 hours. Decorate with whipped double cream. *Serves 6.*

## Lemon curd cloud

8 oz./225 g. lemon curd (see page 47)
¼ pint/1½ dl. single cream
2 egg whites, stiffly beaten

Stir the lemon curd into the cream until well blended, then fold in the egg whites.

**To freeze:** Pack in individual plastic dishes. Seal and freeze.

**To prepare for serving:** De-frost and serve with sponge fingers or langue du chat biscuits. *Serves 4.*

**Note:** The desserts can be served decorated with grated plain chocolate or a sprinkling of nutmeg.

## Lemon soufflé

4 tablespoons cornflour
6 eggs, separated
1 lb. 2 oz./500 g. castor sugar
1½ pints/scant litre milk
6 lemons
¾ oz./20 g. gelatine, dissolved in
   9 tablespoons hot water

Blend the cornflour, egg yolks and sugar with a little of the cold milk. Put the remaining milk on to heat with the lemon rind, pared into thin strips. When the milk is almost boiling, strain off the lemon rind and pour the milk on to the blended cornflour, while stirring. Return the mixture to the pan, bring to the boil, and cook for 3 minutes, stirring all the time. Pour the mixture into a large bowl. Stir in the dissolved gelatine and juice from the lemons. Leave to cool. Whisk the egg whites until stiff. Fold into the cooled mixture.

**To freeze:** Pour into a suitable plastic container and leave in a cool place to set. Cover and freeze.

**To prepare for serving:** Remove the covering and thaw at room temperature allowing approximately 5 hours. Dip the base of the container into warm water and unmould on to a flat plate. Decorate with whipped cream. *Serves 8.*

## Chocolate ice cream

4 oz./100 g. margarine

6 oz./175 g. castor sugar

6 oz./175 g. plain chocolate

4 eggs, separated

½ teaspoon vanilla essence

½ pint/3 dl. evaporated milk, scalded

Cream the margarine and sugar until light and fluffy. Melt the chocolate in a basin over hot water. Stir the chocolate into the egg yolk, add the vanilla essence and creamed mixture.

Whisk the evaporated milk and fold into the chocolate mixture. Pour into a plastic container, cover and freeze for 1 hour. Remove from the freezer and mash with a fork. Whisk the egg whites stiffly and fold into the mixture. Seal and return to the freezer. *Serves 6.*

## Coffee ice cream charlotte

1 tablespoon apricot jam, sieved

19 Boudoir biscuits

*For the coffee ice cream:*

4 eggs, separated

4 oz./100 g. icing sugar, sieved

4 tablespoons bottled coffee essence

3 tablespoons rum

½ pint/3 dl. double cream, lightly whipped

Brush the sides of a 6-inch (15-cm.) cake tin with warmed apricot jam. Trim the biscuits to the depth of the tin then stand round the sides of the tin so they fit closely. Whisk the egg whites until very stiff, then gradually whisk in the icing sugar. Whisk the egg yolks, coffee essence and rum together then whisk gradually into the egg whites. Fold in the cream.

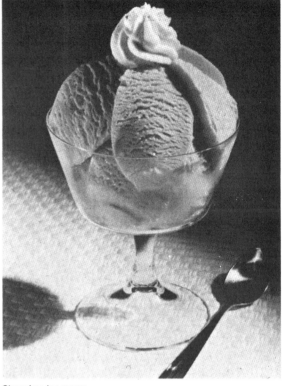

Chocolate ice cream

**To freeze:** Pour into the middle of the cake tin and freeze in the tin with the top tightly covered with foil.

**To prepare for serving:** Carefully loosen round the sides of the tin with a palette knife, then dip the bottom of the tin quickly in warm water. Turn out on to a serving plate. Decorate the top with whipped cream and toasted almonds. *Serves 6–8.*

## Lemon sorbet

8 oz./225 g. granulated sugar

1 pint/6 dl. water

2 lemons

1 egg white

Dissolve the sugar in the water over a gentle heat. Pare the rind thinly from one of the lemons and add it to the sugar. Boil rapidly for 10 minutes, to form a light syrup. Strain into a mixing bowl, allow to cool, add the strained juice of both lemons and freeze for 2 hours. Remove the sorbet from the freezer and whisk to break down the ice particles. Whisk the egg white stiffly and fold into the sorbet.

**To freeze:** Spoon the mixture into a 1½-pint (1-litre) container. Cover closely with foil and re-freeze.

**To prepare for serving:** Serve in scoops while still frozen. *Serves 6.*

## Strawberry cream torte

5 egg whites
pinch cream of tartar
8 oz./225 g. castor sugar
2 oz./50 g. flaked almonds, browned
*For the filling:*
1 tablespoon gelatine dissolved in
   2 tablespoons hot water
½ pint/3 dl. double cream
½ pint/3 dl. single cream
1 tablespoon castor sugar
3 tablespoons Curaçao
1 lb./450 g. fresh strawberries, sliced

Grease and flour two baking sheets. Trace two 6-inch (15-cm.) circles on each. Pre-heat the oven to 225°F., 110°C., Gas Mark ¼.

Whisk the egg whites and cream of tartar until fluffy, add a third of the sugar and continue to whisk until stiff. Add another third of the sugar and whisk until the mixture is shiny and heavy. Fold in the remaining sugar. Spread the mixture evenly within the traced circles and sprinkle with flaked almonds. Cook in the bottom of the oven for 2–3 hours or until crisp. Remove from the baking sheet and cool on a wire tray.

Dissolve the gelatine in the water and leave to set. Whisk the double and single cream until thick enough to leave a trail. Melt the gelatine in a small saucepan, without boiling; mix into the cream with the sugar and the Curaçao. Stir until on the point of setting. Sandwich the meringues together, with cream and strawberries between each layer, reserving some cream to coat the sides and top of the torte.

**To freeze:** Place on a baking sheet and partially freeze in order to set the cream before over-wrapping with sheet polythene.

**To prepare for serving:** Unwrap and serve frozen. *Serves 6–8.*

## Frozen Christmas pudding

*For the one-stage chocolate cake:*
2 oz./50 g. luxury margarine
2 oz./50 g. castor sugar
2 tablespoons rum (optional)
2 oz./50 g. self-raising flour sifted with
   ½ teaspoon baking powder
1 heaped tablespoon cocoa blended with
   1 tablespoon hot water
1 large egg
*For the ice cream:*
2 oz./50 g. castor sugar
¾ oz./20 g. gelatine dissolved in
   4 tablespoons water
1 16-oz./454-g. can evaporated milk, chilled
¼ teaspoon almond essence
2 oz./50 g. glacé cherries, halved
little red colouring
2 oz./50 g. sultanas and currants, mixed
2 teaspoons lemon juice
grated rind of 1 lemon

To make the cake, put all the ingredients into a bowl and beat with a wooden spoon for about 3 minutes. Put into a greased and lined 7-inch (18-cm.) sandwich tin and bake in the centre of a very moderate oven (325°F., 170°C., Gas Mark 3) for 25–30 minutes. Remove from the tin and cool.

While the cake is cooling, prepare the ice cream. Add the sugar and dissolved gelatine to the chilled milk, whisk and put in the refrigerator until just beginning to set. Whisk again and divide in half. Add the almond essence and cherries to one half, then colour pink. Add the remaining ingredients to other half. Pour the pink mixture into a 3-pint (1¾-litre) pudding basin, cover with the cake. Put the other ice cream on top.

**To freeze:** Cover the top of the basin with foil and seal.

**To prepare for serving:** Put the basin into hot water for about 1 minute, remove the foil lid, invert and turn on to a serving plate. Decorate with holly and serve with whipped cream, topped with cinnamon.

For smaller parties, cook the cake mixture in two 5-inch (13-cm.) tins for 20 minutes. Divide the ice cream mixture between two 1½-pint (1-litre) bowls. Serve one pudding and store the other in the freezer.

## Apple and chocolate flan

5 oz./150 g. butter
5 oz./150 g. castor sugar
2 large eggs, well beaten
4 oz./100 g. plain flour
1 oz./25 g. cocoa powder
1 teaspoon baking powder
pinch salt
¼ pint/1½ dl. milk

Cream together the butter and sugar until light and fluffy. Gradually beat in the eggs. Sieve together the flour, cocoa powder, baking powder and salt and fold into the sponge mixture. Stir in the milk and turn into a greased 8½-inch (21-cm.) flan tin. Bake in a moderately hot oven (375°F., 190°C., Gas Mark 5) for 45 minutes or until the sponge is firm to the touch. Cool on a wire tray.

**To freeze:** Wrap closely in foil and freeze.

**To prepare for serving:** Thaw, covered, at room temperature allowing approximately 3 hours. Poach partially thawed apple slices in a sugar syrup until tender. Drain and cool. Just before serving, fill the centre of the flan with scoops of ice cream, top with poached apple slices and decorate with grated chocolate. *Serves 6.*

## Strawberry soufflé

12 oz./350 g. fresh strawberries
castor sugar
½ oz./15 g. gelatine dissolved in ¼ pint/1½ dl. cold water
4 eggs, separated
red colouring
¼ pint/1½ dl. double cream, lightly whipped

Tie a greased, double thickness band of greaseproof paper round a 6-inch (15-cm.) soufflé dish. Hull and wash the strawberries. Sieve or put into a blender and sweeten the purée to taste. Put the gelatine and water in a basin over a pan of gently simmering water until the gelatine has dissolved.

Whisk the egg yolks with 3 oz. (75 g.) sugar over a pan of gently simmering water until thick and creamy. Remove from the heat and whisk until cool. Stir in the gelatine and strawberry purée and colour with a little red colouring to give a good pink colour. When the mixture is thick but not set, fold in the whipped cream. Stiffly whisk the egg whites and fold into the mixture. Turn into the prepared soufflé dish. Put in the freezer and partially freeze.

**To freeze:** Remove the greaseproof collar, using a knife dipped in hot water, if necessary. Cover with polythene tissue paper, seal and replace in the freezer.

**To prepare for serving:** Allow to thaw in the refrigerator for 24 hours. Decorate with whipped cream and strawberries. *Serves 6.*

## Apple and blackcurrant mould

½ pint/3 dl. double cream
½ pint/3 dl. frozen apple purée, thawed
1 egg, separated
1 oz./25 g. gelatine
¼ pint plus 4 tablespoons/2 dl. water
1 lb./450 g. blackcurrants
sugar to taste
1 dessertspoon cornflour

Whip the cream until thick enough to leave a trail then fold into the apple purée, with the stiffly beaten egg white. Dissolve ½ oz. (15 g.) of the gelatine in 2 tablespoons water, heat gently to melt, pour into the apple mixture and stir until on the point of setting. Pour into a large mould and place a small mould of the same shape in the centre. Place in the refrigerator and allow to set before removing the smaller mould.

Meanwhile, simmer the blackcurrants in ¼ pint (1½ dl.) water with sufficient sugar to taste. Blend the cornflour with a little of the juice, add to the blackcurrants, bring to the boil and simmer for 1 minute, stirring constantly. Cool and beat in the egg yolk. Allow the mixture to become completely cold.

Dissolve the remaining gelatine in the rest of the water and heat gently to melt. Add to the blackcurrant mixture and stir until on the point of setting. Pour into the mould and return to the refrigerator to set.

**To freeze:** Seal tightly with double or heavy duty foil and freeze.

**To prepare for serving:** Thaw overnight in the refrigerator. Cut into slices and serve with Boudoir biscuits. *Serves 6–8.*

Chocolate cake with pears and chocolate sauce

## Chocolate cake with pears and chocolate sauce

3 oz./75 g. Savoy fingers or dry sponge cake

1 oz./25 g. plain chocolate

4 oz./100 g. castor sugar

2 eggs, separated

2 tablespoons milk

½ oz./15 g. gelatine

1 oz./25 g. butter

½ teaspoon vanilla essence or 1 teaspoon rum

2 dessert pears, peeled and cored

Use either an ice tray about 7–8 inches (18–20 cm.) long or a 1-lb. (450-g.) loaf tin (the shallow aluminium type). Cut a piece of non-stick lining paper to line the bottom and sides of the tin and give sufficient length to fold over the finished mixture.

Split the Savoy fingers or cut the sponge cake into thin slices. Put a layer in the bottom of the prepared tray, with the rounded sides of the Savoy

fingers next to the paper. Keep the remaining pieces for the top.

Melt the chocolate in a basin over hot water or in a saucepan over a gentle heat. Add half the sugar, the egg yolks and the gelatine dissolved in the milk and continue cooking over a gentle heat stirring all the time, until the mixture thickens. Cool, stirring occasionally.

Cream together the butter and remaining sugar until soft and light. Add to the chocolate mixture and combine thoroughly. Add the vanilla essence or rum. Beat the egg whites until stiff and fold them into the mixture. Pour it into the prepared tray and put another layer of fingers or cake on top. Fold over the spare paper to cover the top. Peel the pears, halve and remove the cores. Poach the pears in heavy sugar syrup until tender.

**To freeze:** Cover the cake with double or heavy duty foil. Seal and freeze. Cool the pears quickly and put into a plastic container, leaving a ½-inch (1-cm.) headspace; cover with crumpled foil to keep the pears submerged. Cover and freeze.

**To serve:** Thaw in the refrigerator for 12 hours and turn out the cake while still slightly chilled. Top with the pears and pour over Dark chocolate sauce (see page 22). *Serves 6.*

## Banana cream

6 bananas

¼ pint/1½ dl. double cream, lightly whipped

¼ pint/1½ dl. thick custard (1 tablespoon custard powder to ¼ pint/1½ dl. milk)

¼ teaspoon vanilla essence

juice of ½ lemon

2 oz./50 g. castor sugar

½ oz./15 g. gelatine dissolved in

¼ pint/1½ dl. hot water

Mash the bananas to a purée with a fork. Blend the banana, whipped cream and cold custard. Add the vanilla essence, lemon juice and gelatine. Whisk until on the point of setting.

**To freeze:** Pour into a plastic or foil container. Cover closely and freeze.

**To prepare for serving:** Thaw at room temperature for approximately 4 hours. *Serves 6.*

# Chapter Six

# Making more of frozen convenience foods

There seems to be something compulsive about the cooking instructions given on frozen food packs. Most housewives follow the instructions to the letter and would never think of combining the contents of one of these handy packets with other ingredients to produce a more interesting finished dish. Yet there are so many appetising dishes you can prepare using ready-frozen products. For example, your own home-made sweet-and-sour sauce, frozen in small quantities, goes beautifully with crispy cod fries, chicken portions or prawns. Add a big dish of fluffy boiled rice or fried rice and you have a really exotic meal. Even an everyday pleasure like a small tub of mousse can be turned into a party sweet with a crown of piped cream and some fruit.

All the recipes given in this chapter were tested in the experimental kitchens of Birds Eye, the largest supplier of frozen foods in this country. They now run a bulk delivery service of their products to home freezer owners.

## Trout amandine

4 frozen trout, 5–6 oz./150–175 g. each
seasoned flour
3 oz./75 g. butter
2 oz./50 g. blanched almonds
juice of ½ lemon
seasoning
*To garnish:*
lemon
parsley

Remove the eyes from the frozen trout and coat the fish in seasoned flour. Melt the butter in a pan and fry the trout for 7 minutes on either side. Remove from the pan, drain and keep warm on a serving dish. Cut the almonds into shreds, toss in the pan and cook them slowly until they are golden brown. Add the lemon juice and seasoning and pour over the fish. Serve garnished with lemon and parsley. *Serves 4.*

## Salmon with cucumber sauce

4 frozen salmon steaks, 4–5 oz./100–150 g. each
½ pint/3 dl. water
1 teaspoon lemon juice
little milk
1 oz./25 g. butter
1 small onion, finely chopped
½ cucumber, peeled and cut into ¼-inch/½-cm. cubes
1 oz./25 g. flour
seasoning
*To garnish:*
cucumber slices
watercress

Poach the frozen steaks in the water and lemon juice for 12–15 minutes. Remove from the pan and drain, reserving the liquor. Remove the skin and bone from the steaks and place on a serving dish; keep warm. Make up the fish liquor to ½ pint (3 dl.) with a little milk. Melt the butter in a saucepan, fry the onion until transparent, add the cucumber and cook for a further 3 minutes. Stir in the flour, cook for 1 minute. Remove from the heat and blend in the fish liquor and milk. Bring the sauce to the boil, stirring, and cook for 3 minutes. Season to taste. Garnish the steaks with cucumber slices and watercress and serve with the sauce. *Serves 4.*

## Cheesy fish fingers

1 12-oz./340-g. packet frozen fish fingers
2 oz./50 g. cheese, grated
1 teaspoon made mustard
1 tablespoon chopped parsley
1 oz./25 g. butter, melted
salt and pepper

Grill the fish fingers on one side for 5 minutes. Meanwhile, mix the cheese, mustard, parsley, butter and seasonings in a bowl. Turn the fish fingers and spread some of the mixture on each fish finger. Grill for a further 5 minutes and serve. *Serves 4–6*.

## Kipper pizzas

*For the dough:*
½ oz./15 g. fresh yeast or 2 teaspoons dried yeast and
    1 teaspoon sugar
½ pint/3 dl. warm milk
8 oz./225 g. plain flour
½ teaspoon salt
½ oz./15 g. butter or margarine
1 small egg, beaten
*For the filling:*
oil
1 11-oz./312-g. packet frozen buttered kipper fillets,
    cooked as instructions
1 1 lb. 12-oz./794-g. can tomatoes, drained
pinch mixed herbs
6 oz./175 g. Cheddar cheese, grated
6 gherkins

If using fresh yeast, blend with the warm milk. If using dried yeast, dissolve the sugar in the milk, sprinkle on the dried yeast and leave for 10 minutes until frothy.

Sift the flour and salt into a large mixing bowl and rub in the butter or margarine. Mix the yeast liquid and beaten egg together. Make a well in the centre of the flour and pour in the milk and yeast mixture. Mix to a firm dough (until the sides of the bowl are clean). Leave the dough in the bowl in a warm place for 30 minutes, cover with a damp cloth and leave until the dough doubles its size.

Divide the dough into six pieces. Knead each piece and roll out into 5-inch (13-cm.) circles. Place on oiled baking sheets and brush with oil. Skin and flake the cooked kippers. Cover the circles with a layer of tomato mixed with the herbs, then with a layer of flaked kipper and top each with 1 oz. (25 g.) grated cheese. Garnish with slices of gherkin and leave in a warm place for 10 minutes to rise a little. Bake in a moderately hot oven (400°F., 200°C., Gas Mark 6) for 18–20 minutes. Serve hot. *Makes 6 individual pizzas*.

Crispy cod fries with
sweet and sour sauce

## Crispy cod fries with sweet and sour sauce

2-inch/5-cm. piece cucumber, diced
2 medium carrots, cut into strips
½ pint/3 dl. pineapple juice
2 tablespoons white vinegar
5 tablespoons brown sugar
2 teaspoons soy sauce
1 tablespoon cornflour, blended with 2 tablespoons water
1 7-oz./198-g. packet frozen crispy cod fries

Cook the cucumber and carrots in boiling, salted water for 5 minutes, drain.

Place the pineapple juice, vinegar and sugar in a pan and heat gently until the sugar has dissolved. Add the soy sauce and blended cornflour and bring to the boil, stirring. Cook for 3 minutes. Add the cucumber and carrot. Cook the crispy cod fries according to the instructions and serve immediately with the sauce. *Serves 4*.

## Cod steak crisps

4 large slices lean bacon
1 14-oz./396-g. packet frozen cod steaks
1 egg, beaten with 1 tablespoon water
4 oz./100 g. potato crisps, finely crushed
oil or fat for frying

Remove the rind from the bacon and flatten with the back of a knife. Wrap one rasher around each cod steak. Dip into the egg and water, then coat in the potato crisps. Press well so that the coating remains firm. Shallow fry the fish for 20 minutes, in fat or oil, turning occasionally. Drain and serve immediately. *Serves 4*.

## Beef Wellington

1 13-oz./368-g. packet frozen puff pastry, thawed
*For the filling:*
2 lb./900 g. fillet of beef, cut in one piece
2 oz./50 g. butter
4 oz./100 g. button mushrooms, sliced
2 teaspoons chopped fresh mixed herbs
beaten egg

Trim the fillet and tie up. Melt the butter in a pan and quickly brown the fillet on all sides. Remove from the pan and allow to cool. Fry the mushrooms in the pan for a few minutes and add the herbs; allow to cool.

Roll out the pastry to a rectangle. Mark the pastry lightly into three and cut off one-third. Spread the mushroom mixture on the larger piece, place the beef on top and press the pastry up round it. Damp the edges of the other piece of pastry and place on top. Seal the edges, brush with beaten egg and decorate with 'leaves' made from pastry trimmings. Bake in a hot oven (425°F., 220°C., Gas Mark 7) for 35–40 minutes, or until well browned. Serve immediately. *Serves 6–8.*

## Chicken vol-au-vent

1 13-oz./368-g. packet frozen puff pastry, thawed
1 beaten egg
*For the filling:*
2 5-oz./150-g. frozen chicken quarters, cooked as
    instructions
$\frac{1}{4}$ pint/1$\frac{1}{2}$ dl. cold white sauce
2 tablespoons mayonnaise
seasoning
1 teaspoon chopped parsley
*To garnish:*
parsley

Roll out the pastry and cut into circles with a 2-inch (5-cm.) cutter. Brush half of these with a little water and place on a damp baking sheet. Mark the remaining circles with a 1-inch (2$\frac{1}{2}$-cm.) cutter and place them on top of the circles on the baking sheet. Press gently together. Glaze with beaten egg and bake in a hot oven (425°F., 220°C., Gas Mark 7) for 10–12 minutes until risen and golden brown. Remove from the baking sheet and allow to cool. Remove the 1-inch (2$\frac{1}{2}$-cm.) 'lids'

Chicken vol-au-vent

from the centre of each.

Allow the cooked chicken to cool, remove the meat from the bones and chop. Blend with the remaining ingredients and pile into the pastr cases. Top with the 'lids' and serve, garnishe with parsley. *Makes 20–22.*

## Coq au vin

1 oz./25 g. butter
1 tablespoon olive oil
6 oz./175 g. button onions
4 oz./100 g. bacon, cut into strips
4 5-oz./150-g. frozen chicken quarters, thawed
5 tablespoons brandy
1 oz./25 g. flour
$\frac{3}{4}$ pint/4 dl. red wine
$\frac{1}{2}$ pint/3 dl. stock
4 oz./100 g. button mushrooms
1 bay leaf
1 teaspoon sugar
salt and freshly milled black pepper
*To garnish:*
fried croûtons

Melt the butter in a flameproof casserole, add th oil and cook the onions with the bacon until th onions are golden brown. Remove and keep on plate. Fry the chicken until lightly browned c both sides, add the brandy and set alight. Whe the flame dies down, remove the chicken on to th plate, add the flour and cook for 2 minute Gradually add the red wine and stock stirring a the time.

Replace the chicken with the onions and bacon. Add the mushrooms, bay leaf, sugar and seasonings. Place the casserole in a warm oven (325°F., 170°C., Gas Mark 3) for 1 hour. Serve garnished with croûtons round the dish.    *Serves 4*

Corn and bacon tarts

Steaklet kebabs

## Steaklet kebabs

1 small green pepper
1 11-oz./312-g. packet frozen steaklets
8 rashers streaky bacon, cut in half and rolled
8 button mushrooms
8 small onions, parboiled
8 small tomatoes, cut in half
oil

Remove the core and seeds from the pepper and cut the flesh into pieces approximately 1 inch (2½ cm.) square. Cut each steaklet into four and arrange alternately with the other ingredients on eight small skewers. Brush with oil and grill gently for 10–15 minutes, turning frequently. Serve hot.    *Serves 4 or 8.*

## Corn and bacon tarts

1 7½-oz./212-g. packet frozen shortcrust pastry, thawed
*For the filling:*
2 eggs
½ onion, grated
1 6-oz./170-g. packet frozen sweetcorn
1 tablespoon chopped parsley
salt and pepper
3 rashers streaky bacon

Roll out the pastry and cut into circles using a 3-inch (7½-cm.) cutter. Put into patty tins. Put the eggs, onion, sweetcorn, parsley and seasoning into a basin. Mix well and spoon into the pastry cases. Snip the bacon into small pieces and place on top of the filling. Bake in a moderately hot oven (375°F., 190°C., Gas Mark 5) for 25–30 minutes. Remove from the patty tins and serve hot or cold. *Makes 18.*

## Souper sausages

6 oz./175 g. spaghetti
1½-oz./40 g. butter
1 onion, finely chopped
1 10-oz./283-g. packet frozen skinless pork sausages,
    cut in ½-inch/1-cm. pieces
1 10-oz./283-g. can condensed tomato soup
few drops Worcestershire sauce
*To garnish:*
chopped parsley

Cook the spaghetti in boiling, salted water for about 12–15 minutes, drain, toss in ½ oz. (15 g.) of the butter and keep warm on a flat serving dish. Meanwhile, melt the rest of the butter in a pan, add the onion and cook until transparent, but not browned, for about 5 minutes. Add the sausages and cook for a further 5 minutes. Stir in the soup and Worcestershire sauce, heat through and pour the mixture over the spaghetti. Garnish with chopped parsley.    *Serves 3–4.*

## Beefburger bean bake

1 16-oz./454-g. can baked beans
1 oz./25 g. butter or margarine
1 8-oz./226-g. packet frozen beefburgers
1 large onion, sliced
4 oz./100 g. button mushrooms

Place the baked beans in an ovenproof dish.
Melt the butter or margarine, add the beefburgers with the onion and mushrooms and fry
gently for 5 minutes turning the beefburgers
once. Remove the beefburgers, place on beans.

Cook the vegetables for a further 3 minutes,
then drain. Place the mushrooms on the beef-
burgers and the onion rings on the mushrooms.
Bake in a moderately hot oven (375°F., 190°C.,
Gas Mark 5) for 15–20 minutes. Serve at once.
*Serves 3–4.*

## Salade niçoise

1 8-oz./226-g. packet frozen sliced green beans
salt
1 15-oz./425-g. can new potatoes, drained
1 7-oz./198-g. can tuna fish, flaked
1 2-oz./57-g. can anchovy fillets, drained and soaked
   in milk
few stoned black olives
4 tablespoons olive oil
2 tablespoons vinegar
pinch pepper
pinch dry mustard
8 oz./225 g. small tomatoes, skinned

Salade niçoise

Cook the beans in boiling, salted water for
5 minutes, drain and cool under running cold
water. Cut the potatoes into ½-inch (1-cm.) cubes,
mix with the beans and tuna and arrange in a
shallow dish. Arrange a lattice of anchovy fillets
on top and place the black olives between the
lattice. Blend together the oil, vinegar and seasonings and spoon over the salad. Cut the tomatoes
into quarters, remove the seeds and arrange
around the dish. *Serves 6.*

## Primavera salad

1 8-oz./226-g. packet frozen broad beans
2 oz./50 g. sliced cooked ham
6 tablespoons olive oil
2 tablespoons vinegar
1 teaspoon lemon juice
pinch salt
pinch black pepper
pinch dry mustard
½ teaspoon sugar
1 lettuce
*To garnish:*
chopped parsley

Cook the beans in boiling, salted water for
7 minutes, drain and cool in running cold water.
Cut the ham into strips 1 inch (2½ cm.) long and
mix with the beans. Blend together the oil,
vinegar, lemon juice, seasonings and sugar. Pour
over the beans and ham and mix together. Wash
and dry the lettuce and arrange on a plate. Top
with the bean and ham mixture and sprinkle with
chopped parsley. *Serves 4–6.*

## Prawn salad

1 lettuce
1 8-oz./226-g. packet frozen peeled prawns, thawed
¼ pint/1½ dl. mayonnaise
*To garnish:*
chopped parsley
lemon slices

Wash and dry the lettuce. Arrange in a shallow
dish and pile the prawns on top, reserving a few
for garnish. Coat with mayonnaise, and decorate
with chopped parsley, prawns and lemon slices.
*Serves 6–8.*

# Rice salad

4 oz./100 g. Patna rice
1 4-oz./113-g. packet frozen diced carrots and peas
1 oz./25 g. blanched almonds
3 tablespoons olive oil
1 tablespoon vinegar
1 tablespoon chopped onion
salt and pepper

Cook the rice in boiling, salted water for about 15 minutes until just tender. Drain and cool in running cold water. Cook the carrots and peas in boiling, salted water for 7 minutes, drain and cool in running cold water. Cut the almonds into shreds. Mix the vegetables with the rice and almonds. Blend together the oil and vinegar and stir in the onion and seasoning. Fold the dressing into the salad and serve. *Serves 4.*

# Tourangelle

¼ pint/1½ dl. double cream
¼ pint/1½ dl. thick mayonnaise
grated rind and juice of ½ lemon
pinch salt
pinch pepper
pinch dry mustard
12 oz./350 g. new potatoes
1 8-oz./226-g. packet frozen French beans
1 large cooking apple, peeled and sliced
*To garnish:*
watercress

Stir the cream into the mayonnaise, gradually add the grated rind and juice of the lemon and season well. Scrub the potatoes and boil them in their skins. Cool, peel and cut into ½-inch (1-cm.) cubes. Cut the frozen beans into 1-inch (2½-cm.) pieces and cook for 5 minutes in boiling, salted water. Drain and cool under running cold water. Place the potatoes, beans and apple in a serving dish, mix with a little of the lemon mayonnaise and top with the remainder. Garnish with watercress. *Serves 5–6.*

# Cheese twists

1 13-oz./368-g. packet frozen puff pastry, thawed
4 oz./100 g. hard Cheddar cheese, grated

Roll out the pastry to a rectangle measuring about 12 by 15 inches (30 by 38 cm.). Sprinkle the grated cheese on top and fold the pastry into three, so that the cheese is layered between the pastry. Roll out again until the pastry measures about 10 by 12 inches (25 by 30 cm.) and cut into thin strips, ¼ by 4 inches (½ by 10 cm.). Twist each of these and space out on damp baking sheets. Bake in a hot oven (425°F., 220°C., Gas Mark 7) for 8–10 minutes until risen and golden. Remove from the baking sheet, cool and serve. *Makes about 100.*

# Raspberry soufflé

1 8-oz./226-g. packet frozen raspberries, thawed
2 oz./50 g. icing sugar
½ oz./15 g. gelatine dissolved in ¼ pint/1½ dl. water
3 eggs, separated
3 oz./75 g. castor sugar
¼ pint/1½ dl. double cream, lightly whipped

Tie a greased, double thickness sheet of grease-proof paper round a 6-inch (15-cm.) soufflé dish. Sieve the raspberries, reserving a few for garnish, and fold the icing sugar into the purée. Heat the gelatine in the water, over a pan of boiling water, and allow to cool slightly. Whisk the egg yolks and castor sugar together over hot water. Fold in the raspberry purée and gelatine, and cool. Fold in half the cream. Whisk the egg whites and fold into the mixture. Turn into the prepared soufflé dish and leave to set. When set, remove the 'collar' carefully and decorate with the remaining whipped cream and raspberries. *Serves 6.*

# Strawberry and hazelnut torte

5 oz./150 g. plain flour
3 oz./75 g. butter or margarine
3½ oz./90 g. castor sugar
2 oz./50 g. hazelnuts, coarsely chopped
1 8-oz./226-g. packet frozen strawberries
½ pint/3 dl. double cream, lightly whipped

Sieve the flour, rub in the butter or margarine. Fold in half the sugar and the nuts and knead the mixture together. Divide the mixture in half and press into two 7-inch (18-cm.) circles on a well greased baking sheet. Bake in a moderately hot oven (375°F., 190°C., Gas Mark 5) for 15–20 minutes or until golden brown. Allow to cool. Meanwhile sprinkle the strawberries with the remaining sugar and allow to thaw for about 1 hour. Reserve a few strawberries for decoration. Spread half the cream on one of the circles, place the fruit on the cream and cover with the second circle. Pipe the remaining cream on top and decorate with the remaining strawberries. *Serves 5–6.*

# Florida cheesecake

*For the crust:*
2 oz./50 g. butter
1 oz./25 g. castor sugar
4 oz./100 g. digestive biscuits, crushed with a rolling pin
*For the filling:*
2 eggs, separated
2 oz./50 g. castor sugar
1 tablespoon undiluted frozen orange juice, thawed
8 oz./225 g. cottage cheese
$\frac{1}{2}$ pint/3 dl. double cream, lightly whipped
*To decorate:*
fresh orange segments
whipped cream

Melt the butter in a pan, add the sugar and crushed biscuits and mix well together. Line an 8-inch (20-cm.) sandwich tin with foil. Press the biscuit mixture into the tin with a spoon and leave in the refrigerator to set.

Beat the egg yolks and sugar together, in a bowl over hot water, until thick and creamy. Add the undiluted orange juice. Allow to cool. Mash the cheese with a fork and add to the mixture. Fold in the cream. Stiffly whisk the egg whites and fold into the mixture. Pour into the crumb base. Fold over the foil and freeze the cake until firm. Decorate with fresh orange segments and whipped cream. Eat semi-frozen. *Serves 6.*

# Cold orange soufflé

3 small eggs, separated
2 oz./50 g. castor sugar
half 6$\frac{1}{4}$-oz./177-g. can undiluted frozen orange juice, thawed
2 tablespoons Cointreau
1 teaspoon lemon juice
$\frac{1}{2}$ oz./15 g. gelatine dissolved in 2 tablespoons water
$\frac{1}{4}$ pint/1$\frac{1}{2}$ dl. double cream, lightly whipped
*To decorate:*
whipped cream
angelica
fresh orange segments or nuts

Tie a greased, double thickness sheet of grease-proof paper round a 5-inch (13-cm.) soufflé dish. Beat the egg yolks with the sugar, in a bowl over a pan of boiling water, until thick and creamy. Remove from the heat and continue to whisk for a further few minutes. Whisk in the orange juice, Cointreau and lemon juice.

Melt the gelatine in the water in a small bowl over a pan of hot water, stir into the mixture. Fold in the cream. Stiffly whisk the egg whites and fold into the mixture. Turn the orange mixture into the prepared soufflé dish and leave to set. When set, remove the 'collar' carefully and decorate with whipped cream, angelica, fresh orange segments or nuts if liked. *Serves 4–5.*

# Florida orange jelly

1 6$\frac{1}{4}$-oz./177-g. can frozen undiluted orange juice, thawed
2 cans water
$\frac{1}{2}$ oz./15 g. gelatine
1 apple, peeled, cored and roughly diced

Pour the orange juice into a bowl and add 1$\frac{1}{2}$ cans water. Dissolve the gelatine in the remaining $\frac{1}{2}$ can of water in a basin over hot water. Allow to cool. When cooled, add the gelatine to the orange juice with the diced apple. Pour into a mould and leave until set. Turn out and serve slightly chilled if possible. *Serves 4.*

Turn out each mousse carefully while still frozen and lift with a palette knife onto a slice of Swiss roll.

Decorate mousse party special with cream and strawberries.

## Mousse party special

4 thick slices jam Swiss roll
4 strawberry mousse tubs
¼ pint/1½ dl. double cream, lightly whipped
8 oz./225 g. strawberries or raspberries

Place the slices in the centres of four small glass plates. Turn out each mousse carefully while still frozen and lift with a palette knife on to a slice of Swiss roll. Using a rose tube and large forcing bag, pipe cream rosettes round the base of each mousse. Decorate the edge with a few strawberries and place a single strawberry on top of each mousse. *Serves 4.*

**Variation:** To make an interesting change, or when fresh berries are out of season, use a chocolate Swiss roll and chocolate mousse tubs. Decorate in a similar way with whipped cream, chocolate buttons or grated chocolate.

## Tangy apple tart

1 7½-oz./212-g. packet frozen shortcrust pastry, thawed
*For the filling:*
1 oz./25 g. butter
2 oz./50 g. castor sugar
1 egg, beaten
1 teaspoon grated lemon rind
1 tablespoon lemon juice
2 large cooking apples, peeled and coarsely grated

Roll out the pastry and line a 7-inch (18-cm.) flan ring. Melt the butter, remove from the heat and add the remaining ingredients. Spoon the filling into the flan case. Cut the pastry trimmings into strips ¼ inch (½ cm.) wide and make a lattice on the top of the flan. Bake in a moderately hot oven (400°F., 200°C., Gas Mark 6) for about 40 minutes. Serve chilled with cream. *Serves 4.*

## Lemon meringue tartlets

1 7½-oz./212-g. packet frozen shortcrust pastry, thawed
*For the filling:*
1½ oz./45 g. cornflour
½ pint/3 dl. water
grated rind and juice of 1 large lemon
5 oz./150 g. castor sugar
2 eggs, separated

Roll out the pastry and cut into circles using a 3-inch (7½-cm.) cutter. Put into patty tins, prick well and bake 'blind' for 7–10 minutes in a moderate oven (350°F., 180°C., Gas Mark 4). Blend the cornflour with the water, lemon rind and juice, 1 oz. (25 g.) of the sugar and the egg yolks in a saucepan and bring to the boil, stirring. Cook for 3 minutes and spoon into the tarts. Whisk the egg whites until stiff, beat in half the remaining sugar and continue whisking until dry and firm. Fold in the rest of the sugar and pipe or spoon on to the tartlets. Bake in a slow oven (300°F., 150°C., Gas Mark 2) for 20–30 minutes until the meringue is firm. Remove from the patty tins and cool. *Makes 18.*

## Grapefruit zabaione

4 egg yolks
2 oz./50 g. castor sugar
3 tablespoons undiluted frozen grapefruit juice, thawed
2 tablespoons sweet sherry

Beat the egg yolks and sugar together in a bowl over a pan of boiling water until thick and creamy. Remove the bowl from the heat and gradually whisk in the grapefruit juice and sherry. Continue whisking until the mixture is thick again. Serve immediately in glasses or serve chilled with langues de chat. *Serves 6.*

75

## Strawberry éclairs

Allow 2 medium or 3 small strawberries for each éclair. Make a slit in the side of the frozen éclairs and allow to thaw. Cut the strawberries in half and place in the cream inside the éclairs. Serve.

## Orange honeys

2 oz./50 g. butter
2 oz./50 g. sugar
1 tablespoon frozen undiluted orange juice, thawed
1 tablespoon honey or golden syrup
4 oz./100 g. cornflakes

Place the butter, sugar, orange juice and honey in a saucepan, bring to the boil and simmer for 2 minutes only. Gently stir in the cornflakes and mix thoroughly with the syrup. Spoon into paper bun cases and bake in a moderate oven (350°F., 180°C., Gas Mark 4) for 5 minutes. Allow to cool thoroughly before storing in an air-tight tin. *Makes 24–36.*

## Suggestions for planning menus to make the fullest use of the freezer

All the recipes marked with an asterisk are given in this chapter. Use them when you need to plan appetising meals with the minimum of preparation time, using commercially frozen products which the freezer enables you to store in quantity.

## BUFFET LUNCHEON
  Asparagus rolls
★Salade niçoise
★Prawn salad
★Rice salad
★Tourangelle
  Garlic bread
  Chicken joints
★Primavera salad
  Tossed green salad
  Cassata
★Tangy apple tart and cream
★Raspberry soufflé

## BUFFET SUPPER
★Cheese twists
  Sausage rolls

★Chicken vol-au-vent
★Crispy cod fries with sweet and sour sauce
★Steaklet kebabs
★Corn and bacon tarts
★Kipper pizzas
  Sausages in bacon
★Strawberry éclairs
★Lemon meringue tartlets

## FOUR DINNER PARTY MENUS
  Iced consommé
★Salmon with cucumber sauce
  Asparagus
  New potatoes
  Petits pois
★Strawberry and hazelnut torte

★Trout amandine
★Coq au vin
  Broccoli spears
  Potato croquettes
★Florida cheesecake

  Potted shrimps
★Beef Wellington
  Whole green beans
  Duchesse potatoes
★Grapefruit zabaione

  Pâté
  Breaded scampi and tartare sauce
  Chips
  Broccoli spears
★Orange soufflé

## CHILDREN'S HIGH TEA
★Cod steak crisps
★Souper sausages
★Beefburger bean bake
★Cheesy fish fingers
  Crispy cod fries
  Sausage savouries

★Florida orange jelly
★Orange honeys
  Mousse in tubs
  Dairy cream trifle
  Eclairs

# WEEK DAY MEALS

A busy working mother's plan for feeding her family from the freezer on week days, leaving her time for more elaborate cooking at the weekend.

**Monday**
Grilled chicken quarters
Grilled mushrooms
Sweetcorn
New potatoes

Fresh fruit salad and
cream

**Tuesday**
Steak and kidney pie
Mixed vegetables
Mashed potato

Orange lemon tub mousse
with mandarins

**Wednesday**
Braised beef slices
Horseradish sauce
Roast potatoes
Brussels sprouts

Dairy cream trifle

**Thursday**
Chicken and mushroom
casserole
Potato croquettes
Cauliflower

Pears and hot chocolate
sauce

**Friday**
Fish and chips
Tartare sauce
Peas
Grilled tomato halves

Arctic roll and peaches

# USEFUL THAWING TIME-TABLES

## Cakes

| Type | Approx. room temperature thawing time |
|---|---|
| 8-inch layer cake | |
|   1 layer, not iced | $1-1\frac{1}{4}$ hours |
|   2 layer, with $\frac{1}{2}$-inch icing | 2 hours |
|   2 layer, with $\frac{1}{4}$-inch icing | $1-1\frac{1}{4}$ hours |
|   2 layer, with $\frac{1}{8}$-inch icing | $1-1\frac{1}{4}$ hours |
| Angel cake, sponge | |
|   Whole cake | 3–4 hours |
|   Wedges | $1\frac{1}{4}-1\frac{1}{2}$ hours |
| Cupcakes | 12–25 minutes |

## Bread and sandwiches

| Type | Approx. refrigerator thawing time | Approx. room temperature thawing time |
|---|---|---|
| Uncooked bread dough | Overnight | 5–6 hours |
| Baked bread | Overnight | 5–6 hours |
| Baked rolls | Overnight | 2–3 hours |
| Baked bread slices | | 2–3 minutes in toaster or under grill |
| Sandwiches | | $2\frac{1}{2}$–3 hours |
| Canapés | 1–2 hours | 15–20 minutes |

## Dairy foods

| Type | Approx. refrigerator thawing time | Approx. room temperature thawing time |
|---|---|---|
| Eggs, whole | 18–20 hours per $\frac{1}{2}$ pint | $1\frac{1}{2}$ hours |
| Eggs, yolks | 18–20 hours per $\frac{1}{2}$ pint | $1\frac{1}{2}$ hours |
| Cream | 8 hours per $\frac{1}{4}$ lb. | $1\frac{1}{2}$ hours |
| Cheese | 8 hours per $\frac{1}{4}$ lb. | 2–3 hours |
| Butter | 2 hours per $\frac{1}{2}$ lb. | 30 minutes |
| Milk | 18–20 hours per pint | $1\frac{1}{2}$ hours |

## Vegetables

| Type | Approx. refrigerator thawing time | Approx. room temperature thawing time |
|---|---|---|
| Beetroot, young | 9–10 hours per lb. | 2–3 hours |
| Mushroom, caps | 6–8 hours per lb. | 2–3 hours |
| Peppers (sliced) | 24 hours per lb. | $1\frac{1}{2}$ hours |
| Potatoes | 6 hours per lb. | $1\frac{1}{2}$ hours |

# Meat

| Type | Approx. refrigerator thawing time | Approx. room temperature thawing time |
|---|---|---|
| Beef | 5 hours per lb. | 2 hours per lb. |
| Veal | 5 hours per lb. | 2 hours per lb. |
| Lamb | 5 hours per lb. | 2 hours per lb. |
| Pork | 5 hours per lb. | Thaw in refrigerator only as de-frosting in a warm room can be dangerous. |
| Sausages | 6 hours per lb. | 1½–2 hours per lb. |
| Chops (½ inch thick) | 6 hours per lb. | 1–2 hours per lb. |
| Steaks (½ inch thick) | 6 hours per lb. | 1–2 hours per lb. |
| Steaks (1 inch thick) | 8 hours per lb. | 2–3 hours per lb. |
| Steaks (over 1 inch thick) | 8–10 hours per lb. | 3–4 hours per lb. |
| Poultry (whole) | See chart on page 78 for thawing poultry | |
| Chicken (portions) | 5–6 hours per lb. | 1 hour per lb. |
| Minced meat | 10–12 hours per lb. | 1–1½ hours per lb. |
| Meat patties | 6 hours per lb. | 1 hour per lb. |

**Offal**

| Type | Approx. refrigerator thawing time | Approx. room temperature thawing time |
|---|---|---|
| Sheep's heart | 8–9 hours per lb. | 1–1½ hours per lb. |
| Lamb's kidney | 8–9 hours per lb. | 1–1½ hours per lb. |
| Sliced liver | 8–9 hours per lb. | ½–¾ hour per lb. |
| Sliced sweetbreads | 10 hours per lb. | ¾–1 hour per lb. |
| Tripe | 10–12 hours per lb. | 1–1½ hours per lb. |
| Lamb's tongue | 10–12 hours per lb. | 1–1¼ hours per lb. |

**Game**

| Type | Approx. refrigerator thawing time | Approx. room temperature thawing time |
|---|---|---|
| Hare | 5–6 hours per lb. | 1½–2 hours per lb. |
| Rabbit | 5–6 hours per lb. | 1½–2 hours per lb. |
| Cooked meat stews and casseroles | 8–10 hours per lb. | 1–1½ hours per lb. |

# Fish

| Type | Approx. refrigerator thawing time | Approx. room temperature thawing time |
|---|---|---|
| Haddock | 6–10 hours per lb. | 3–5 hours per lb. |
| Halibut | 6–10 hours per lb. | 3–5 hours per lb. |
| Herring | 6–10 hours per lb. | 3–5 hours per lb. |
| Mackerel | 6–10 hours per lb. | 3–5 hours per lb. |
| Salmon | 6–10 hours per lb. | 3–5 hours per lb. |
| Turbot | 6–10 hours per lb. | 3–5 hours per lb. |
| Trout | 6–10 hours per lb. | 3–5 hours per lb. |
| Cod | 6–10 hours per lb. | 3–5 hours per lb. |
| Plaice | 6–10 hours per lb. | 3–5 hours per lb. |
| Sole | 6–10 hours per lb. | 3–5 hours per lb. |
| Whiting | 6–10 hours per lb. | 3–5 hours per lb. |
| Crab | 10–12 hours per pint carton | 3 hours per pint carton |
| Lobster | 10–12 hours per pint carton | 3 hours per pint carton |
| Oysters | 8 hours | 4–6 hours |
| Scallops | 8 hours | 4–6 hours |
| Shrimps | 6–8 hours per 4-oz. pack | 1½–2 hours per pint carton |
| Kippers | 5 hours | 2–2½ hours |
| Smoked haddock | 5 hours | 2–2½ hours |
| Bloaters | 5 hours | 2–2½ hours |

# Poultry

| Type | Approx. refrigerator thawing time |
|---|---|
| Chickens 4 lb. and over | 1–1½ days |
| Under 4 lb. | 12–16 hours |
| Ducks 3–5 lb. | 1–1½ days |
| Geese 4–14 lb. | 1–2 days |
| Turkeys 18 lb. and over | 2–3 days |
| Under 18 lb. | 1–2 days |

# Fruit

| Type | Approx. refrigerator thawing time | Approx. room temperature thawing time |
|---|---|---|
| **Soft fruits** (skinless) | | |
| Blackberries | 6–7 hours | 2–3 hours |
| Raspberries | 6–7 hours | 2–3 hours |
| Strawberries | 6–7 hours | 2–3 hours |
| **Soft fruits** (with tough skins) | | |
| Avocado – whole | 7–8 hours | 3–4 hours |
| Apricots | 7–8 hours | 3–4 hours |
| Cherries | 7–8 hours | 3–4 hours |
| Cranberries | 7–8 hours | 3–4 hours |
| Currants | 7–8 hours | 3–4 hours |

| | | | |
|---|---|---|---|
| Damsons | 7–8 hours | 3–4 hours | |
| Figs | 7–8 hours | 3–4 hours | |
| Gooseberries | 7–8 hours | 3–4 hours | |
| Grapes | 7–8 hours | 3–4 hours | |
| Grapefruit segments | 7–8 hours | 3–4 hours | |
| Peaches | 7–8 hours | 3–4 hours | |
| **Crisp fruits** | | | |
| Apple slices | 7–8 hours | 3½–4 hours | |
| Pear slices | 7–8 hours | 3½–4 hours | |
| Rhubarb | 7–8 hours | 3½–4 hours | |

## Fruit purées

| ½-pint packs | Approx. refrigerator thawing time | Approx. room temperature thawing time |
|---|---|---|
| Apple purée | 6–8 hours | 2–4 hours |
| Avocado purée | 6–8 hours | 2–4 hours |
| Banana purée | 6–8 hours | 2–4 hours |

To thaw fruit juice allow 2–3 hours at room temperature or 4–6 hours in the refrigerator.

**Note:** To convert these thawing time-tables to metric measurements, use the following equivalents: 1 pint equals 568 ml. or roughly 6 dl.; 1 lb. equals approximately 450 g.; 1 inch equals 2·54 cm.

# Index